ADVANCEMENT
THROUGH
SERVICE

A History of
The Frontiers International

Frederick Johnson
and Leonard Bethel

UNIVERSITY
PRESS OF
AMERICA

Lanham • New York • London

Copyright © 1991 by
University Press of America,® Inc.
4501 Forbes Boulevard, Suite 200
Lanham, Maryland 20706
UPA Acquisitions Department (301) 459-3366

Estover Road
Plymouth PL6 7PY
United Kingdom

First paperback edition 2012

British Library Cataloging in Publication Information Available

The cloth edition of this book was previously
cataloged by the Library of Congress as follows:

Johnson, Frederick, 1915-
Advancement through service : a history of the frontiers
International / Frederick Johnson and Leonard Bethel.
p.   cm.
Includes bibliographical references and index.
1.   Frontiers International—History.
2.   I. Bethel, Leonard, 1929- . II. Title.
E185.5.F93J64   1991   369.5-—dc20   91-15265 CIP

ISBN: 978-0-7618-5973-4

ACKNOWLEDGMENTS

We extend our special thanks to the following individuals and agencies who helped in compiling this history:

Mrs. Bertha Allen Mason of Columbus, Ohio, Nimrod Allen's sister, who, at her own expense, "went the second mile" to provide valuable information and documentation.

Ms. Leslie Allen of Long Island, New York, Mr. Allen's great-grandniece, and to Mr. James Allen of Columbus, Ohio, his great-cousin, for opening new avenues of research.

Mr. Thomas Weissinger, formerly Librarian at Rutgers University and now Chief of Library Research at Cornell University, for invaluable material through the nation's college library system, and for providing a list of newspaper libraries in those cities where Frontiers Clubs exist at no cost to Frontiers.

Elmer C. Jackson, Jr., Esq., Frontiers' Legal Counselor, for the four large containers of Frontiers' archive materials he sent at his own expense.

Mr. William Ashby, Nimrod Allen's friend, Yale classmate, and fellow executive in the National Urban League, for helping us to understand the directions and motivations of Allen's life.

Mrs. Thelma E. Robinson of Frontiers National Headquarters for enthusiastically providing us with materials from the archives.

Mr. Andrew Wertz, Frontiers' First District Director, for his encouragement and flashes of brilliance in research technique.

All the Frontiers Clubs who have cooperated fully and who have waited so patiently for the release of this history.

The following newspapers for their cooperation and for holding their expenses to the minimum:

Banner & Tennessean, Nashville, Tennessee; Akron Beacon Journal, Akron, Ohio; Decatur Herald & Review, Decatur, Illinois; St. Louis Post-Dispatch, St. Louis, Missouri; and the Omaha World Herald, Omaha, Nebraska.

And finally, with special emphasis, the strong support of the former International president, Guy E. Jones.

ABOUT THE AUTHORS

Frederick A. Johnson

Chairman, Historical Committee, Frontiers International
Former Editor, FRONTRUNNER, (Newsletter for District I),
Retired Technical Writer/Cataloger, Nuclear Engineering
Directorate, Picatinny Arsenal, Dover, New Jersey
A Charter Yokefellow, and a Past President of the
Plainfield Area Club, Plainfield, New Jersey
Graduate: Thomas A. Edison College. Currently engaged
in Free-Lance Writing
Has been Newspaper Columnist, and has contributed
poems, short stories, and articles to Newspapers, Army
Publications, and National Magazines

Dr. Leonard L. Bethel

Past Chair of Department of African Studies, and
Associate Professor at Rutgers University, New
Brunswick, New Jersey
Pastor, Bethel Presbyterian Church, Plainfield, New
Jersey
Former Vice-Moderator, United Presbyterian Church,
Synod of the North East
Author of several books and numerous magazine articles
In 1974 he was listed in "Who's Who for Community
Leaders of America
In 1975 he was awarded membership in Phi Delta Kappa
Fraternity
In 1978 he became a Paul Robeson Faculty Award Winner
In 1980 he was granted a Presidential Citation from the
National Association for Equal Opportunity in Higher
Education
In 1984 he was selected by the Woodrow Wilson National
Fellowship Foundation of Princeton University to
participate in their summer institute on "Global
Interdependence and New Jersey Education."
In 1984 --Appointed by Governor Thomas Kean as a member
of the New Jersey Historical Commission.

A Yokefellow of the Plainfield Area Club
Plainfield, New Jersey

TABLE OF CONTENTS

INTRODUCTION

The slavery period in America brought with it the signs of suffering and discontent as experienced by both Black male and female expatriates from the African continent. Using the body of the Black woman as an instrument of reproduction for the slave trade system under what was labelled "slave mongering", was beyond all human compassion. Equally as destructive was the demasculation of the Black male who was constantly treated like an immature child. Long after the Emancipation Proclamation, and even into contemporary times, the stigma of inferiority remained in tact as a tacit reminder that integration was only acceptable under certain circumstances. The social arena was closed to Black participation (i.e. clubs, private and fraternal organizations). Excuses were used to justify the exclusive posture. Black men, for example were labelled as dishonest, disrespectful to their women, and generally a social menace.

Creativity, resourcefulness and a strong vision of equality in America, helped Black men and women to establish their own organizations. The nineteenth century German philosopher Friedrich Nietzsche wrote, "Man's tragedy is that he was once a child. None the less, we cannot afford to forget that, as Charles Odier has shown us, the neurotic's fate remains in his own hands".[1]

In a 1944 pamphlet statement written by a nonprofit educational organization - the Public Affairs Committee, the information presented could have been easily written in today's daily news:

A Negro is not often permitted to be an American first and a Negro second. He is looked on as primarily a Negro. Many Negroes have become prominent, or even famous, but usually as representatives of their race. A Negro economist is always expected to specialize in Negro problems; a Negro lawyer is expected to handle Negro cases; and a Negro trade union leader usually represents Negro workers. Many of the Negroes holding high government posts serve as advisors on Negro affairs. There are no Negro Senators,... and no Negro state governors.[2]

Higher education, emerging as a giant force in the latter 1800's, especially with the establishment of Black colleges, helped many Black men and women to gain the security, both intellectually and monetarily, to render public service to their fellows who suffered from racial discrimination and poverty. "In their roles of teachers, social workers, doctors, and leaders of organizations concerned with the advancement of Negroes," suggested sociologist, E. Franklin Frazier, "the intelligentsia exercise a powerful influence on the ideologies and values of Negroes".[3] It was out of the profile of this group that Frazier allotted to, that men of dedication and a strong concern for service to community grew. They overstepped the social and psychological odds and barriers by receiving either formal education or vocational training which helped to polish their craft and job skills. It was this group who dispelled the negative social myths about Black males not being responsible citizens who gave their volunteer time to render service to the community.

The Frontiers International began as a service organization, national in scope, which has functioned on a local community level. A national office and local clubs across the country constituted the structural format of the organization.

The forerunner of the organization was called "Frontiers of America," and was founded in Columbus, Ohio, on November 10, 1936. Its founder, Nimrod Booker Allen, Executive Secretary of the Columbus, Ohio Urban League in 1936, called together a few men who had concerns about the condition of blacks in America, and began to confront the many problems that faced the minority community. They were unanimous in their concern that an organization be established which could be dedicated to service. As a result, "Frontiers of America" was incorporated in the state of Ohio on December 24, 1938. In 1962 the Frontiers became "International" (and was named "Frontiers International Incorporated") when a charter was granted to a club in British Guiana (now called Guyana).

The Frontiers, historically, has been made up of Black men functioning at local club levels. Men from the business, educational, and professional world were members. They were persons who tended to have a strong commitment to service and a sense for a better way of life for the less fortunate. Its members (including the women's auxiliary) were often members of other nonprofit service organizations such as the YMCA, YWCA, scholarship concerns, United Way, NAACP, Urban League, various fraternities and sororities, and the Big Brother and Big Sister programs.

The strength of the Frontiers International as an organization traditionally rested on the programs, activities, and efforts of the local clubs. It was born in the heart of the Depression years in America. There was racial and religious indifference in the land during the turbulent years of the 1930's; however, the Frontiers managed to maintain a posture of service to the deprived and needy in the minority community. Activities like support for college scholarships, giving blood, finding jobs for the needy, donating reading materials to Black college libraries, providing food for the hungry, are just a few activities endorsed and practiced by Frontiers clubs.

One of the major projects undertaken by the Frontiers in 1950 was the establishment of the first and only national foundation dedicated exclusively to the provision of funds for the research, treatment and cure of vitiligo (a disease which robs its victims of skin color). Projects like this characterized the profile of the Frontiers in the form of service.

Local clubs tended to volunteer service in their own communities which characterized the needs and activities of those areas. Their response always upheld the principles of volunteer service.

Some clubs had organized "Auxiliary Clubs" (collectively called the Coordinating Council) which were made up of the wives and daughters of active or deceased members of the Frontiers.

As the oldest Black service organization in the United States, Frontiers held a unique position. Its history, like that of the NAACP and the Urban League, formed a "spoke in the wheel" that linked together the past and the present in the lives of Black Americans. Like the NAACP and the Urban League, Frontiers established a network of clubs and individuals across the nation. Unlike the latter groups, the Frontiers' main thrust was not political or economic, but was, and still is, to render unselfish community service.

Community service was an intense, never-ending effort to improve the quality of life within a limited area. The history of the Frontiers International, therefore, was the composite history of each of its individual clubs. Their work through the years has been continuously voluntary, dedicatory and exemplary.

Fred Johnson
Leonard Bethel

Notes

[1]Frantz Fanon, <u>Black Skins, White Masks</u> (N.Y. Grove Press, Inc., 1967), p.10.

[2]Maxwell S. Stewart, (N.Y.: Public Affairs Pamphlets, 1944), p.1.

[3E]. Franklin Frazier, <u>Black Bourgeoisie</u>, (N.Y.: Collier Books, 1962), p.84.

CHAPTER I

NIMROD B. ALLEN

"On a raw, cold day (November 10) in 1936 six men sat at lunch in the Monroe Avenue Social Center of the Columbus Urban League (in Columbus, Ohio) and discussed a service club."[1] Among the group were three social workers, two business men, and one dentist. Nimrod B. Allen, Executive Secretary of the Columbus Urban League, had called the meeting. He kept trying to crystalize this new sense of need that was in every man's mind.

"The community desperately needed an organization that could speak and act thoughtfully and without restraint on behalf of Negro citizens."[2] The business and professional men were stagnating for lack of a source of fellowship and inspiration. Something had to be done to continue the community's constant supply of effective leaders. White business and professional men made their civic contributions through their luncheon clubs. Negro men would find value in using a similar instrument of civic expression.

"Nothing much happened in this first meeting, no motions were passed, no resolutions were adopted, nothing was settled, and only one decision reached."[3] That decision was to meet again and continue the discussion. There was a consensus of opinion that this meeting had struck on a tremendously significant idea, if it could be harnessed and translated into words and action.

"For three months the little group continued meeting, discussing, and studying the service club idea."[4] Although a few new members were brought in early in the life of the group, for the three formative months the same little group of men kept trying to think this idea through to their complete satisfaction. In all these meetings they observed religiously the two basic requirements of a service club, namely, (a) regular meetings (b) with luncheon.

"The possibilities of the new idea seemed unlimited, and the need was urgent."[5] They were resolved to make a try. In February 1937 the group formally organized as the Frontiers Club of Columbus, adopted a constitution, and elected officers. In the years ahead they saw a national federation of Negro service clubs, but at this time they were realistic enough to know they must first experiment in a single community. Before they could go to business and professional men anywhere else with this idea, it must have been thoroughly tested, proved sound, and a blueprint of operation developed. Negroes had had far too many unhappy experiences with organizations.

"In 1938, two years after the experiment was begun, the men were certain their idea was sound. This evidenced itself in the organization and chartering of the Frontiers Club of Akron, Ohio, in February 1939, and the Frontiers Club of Cincinnati, Ohio, in July of the same year. However, three other attempts ended in temporary failure. The blueprint of operation was sound, but the technique of organization needed further study and development. With this trilogy of clubs as a nucleus, then, a serious study was made of the technique of selling the Frontiers idea. The result is a sound and tested procedure."[6]

Although the idea sounded new to the five who sat at lunch with him that cold day in 1936, to Nimrod Allen, who had nurtured it, Frontiers was an old idea whose time had come. "The heads of organizations," Allen said, "at work among Negroes lived in a 'no man's land.' If they had the courage to fight for the cause of equal rights for all people, they were in danger of being severely criticized and penalized by both whites and Negroes. To do this, they needed back of them a group of independent persons so that they would not have to stand alone."[7]

Nimrod Booker Allen had already lived a half century when he founded the Frontiers' organization. He was born October 12, 1886, in Girard (now Phoenix City), Alabama, the second youngest son of the 12 children of George Wesley and Phoebe Harvey Allen. Nimrod's father was a minister, an educator, and the editor of the Southern Christian Recorder. It was no accident that Nimrod's middle name was "Booker"for his father, as an Alabama State Legislator during the post civil war Reconstruction Period, had been instrumental in getting a bill passed to build a school where Tuskegee Institute now stands. He was also among those who persuaded Booker T. Washington to come from Hampton Institute in Virginia to head the fledgling Normal School.

"All Negroes in my community," said Allen, "as in most other communities of the South, were psychologically and socially handicapped. I never saw a Negro lawyer, policeman, YMCA worker, stenographer, nurse, social worker, etc., until I came to Ohio--a student at Wilberforce University."[8]

Allen continued, "I have never been to a free school in my whole life. My parents had to pay tuition in the public school. All children paid five cents a week through the third grade, ten cents through the seventh, and fifteen cents a week through the eighth and ninth grades. There was no compulsory school attendance, and the colored people had to raise the money to build the two-room schoolhouse where the Negro children attended."[9]

Allen did not start school until the eighth year. "I was so small physically at 7," he said, "my mother feared I could not hold my own with children my age. When I did start I held my own alright, because I just loved to fight, and because of the quality and quantity of my schoolwork I was permitted to skip grades until I more than caught up with my chronological schedule. The first desk I sat behind with a seat and backrest was bought with money raised by the students. The opportunity was mine to see the need and to head the movement. Previous to that we all sat on benches with no backs.[10]

My smallness in height and weight," Allen continued, "invited physical combat in the uncultured community in which we lived, therefore, I had to learn the art of self-protection. Fighting became second nature to me. It came natural for me to transfer this urge for physical combat for the willingness to face social, psychological, and political conflicts which seem to be inevitable in all group work endeavors."[11]

"There were no public high schools for Negroes in the south," declared Allen. "The public school in Girard went through the ninth grade. After I finished, while waiting two years for my turn to be sent to college, I did one year postgraduate work to get all that the school had to offer me. My high school work was done through the tutoring by my older brothers who had attended such schools as Georgia State Industrial College, Clark University, Tuskegee Institute, and a chance given me because of my previous scholarship record to make up my high school credits while doing my college work. This I was able to do in four years at Wilberforce University."[12]

Allen graduated from Wilberforce University with a B.A. Degree. An Honorary M.A. Degree was bestowed by Wilberforce in 1920. He earned an S.T.B. degree from Yale University in 1915. He was also the recipient of the honorary degree, Doctor of Laws, from Morris Brown College (1953) and from Monrovia College in Monrovia, Liberia (1955).

3

From 1910 - 1912, Nimrod Allen was traveling agent for the Southern Christian Recorder. In 1916 Allen married Clara Elberta Wilson, a marriage that continued until her death in 1966. They had one adopted daughter, Phoebe Jeanette (now Mrs. Phoebe Carter), and three grandchildren: William T. Mattison, Jr., Yvonne Patricia Mattison, and Nimrod Allen Bynum.

From 1915 - 1921, Allen served as Executive Secretary of the Spring Street Branch Y.M.C.A in Columbus, Ohio.

"The Spring Street 'Y'," (wrote A. L. Foster, that institution's Educational Secretary) "was founded in 1912 and was carrying a limited amount of work in a building costing $15,000."

"Nimrod Allen arrived on the scene in 1915. By May 25, 1919, he had spearheaded the building of a $150,000 center to house the Y.M.C.A. Of this amount Mr. Julius Rosenwald donated $25,000, it being the twelfth building erected on the impetus of his generous gifts. It is one of the finest buildings in the United States."[13]

On the first floor was the cafeteria, education rooms, ladies' rest room, barber shop, lockers, businessmen's clubroom, natatorium, showers, and bath. The main floor contained the men's and boys' lobbies, reading rooms, billiard and pool rooms, club rooms, and a fully equipped gymnasium. A suite of offices was also on that floor. The third and fourth floors were used for dormitory purposes. The balcony of the gymnasium was in the form of a running track. The building was modernly equipped in every particular. In the commercial department of the Night School were twelve typewriters representing the leading makes, adding machines, mimeographing machines, and other equipment found in a modern office.

"Mr. Allen divided the membership of the association into clubs. The Businessmen's Club, which, according to Foster, was the only one of its kind in the United States, was composed of the leading business and professional men in the city."[14] At weekly meetings civic and social problems were discussed. The Young Men's Recreation Club was composed of a group of young, wide-awake men who also held regular weekly meetings. The Industrial Men's Club was composed, for the most part, of men who were engaged in the industries and who discussed all phases of industrial work. Special facilities were provided for those clubs and each was touched by every department of the association. The Branch also published a weekly paper known as 'the Association News.' This paper carried the activities of the Association, both local and foreign. Subscription to the News was included in the membership fee, and consequently, the members were kept informed relative to the work of the association. The paper also had a large local circulation among people who were not members.

"With its wide-awake staff determined to play its part in the advancement of the colored citizenry of Columbus," continued Foster, "the Spring Street 'Y' wields a powerful influence in the community."[15]

In 1951, the magazine "Color" which was published in Charleston, West Virginia, stated that "through the efforts of Nimrod Allen the first complete standard YMCA program was begun."

Despite his own spectacular success with his YMCA program, Allen could detect that because of racism, the economic and social condition of blacks in Columbus and throughout the country was steadily worsening. The following paragraph is taken from his article entitled "East Long Street" published in the November 1922 issue of Crisis Magazine:

Mr. Quinlan, a white citizen, in his "Color Line in Ohio," published in 1913, stated "Until quite recently the Negro population of Columbus was considered the most backward of that of the four largest cities in the state. Columbus, the Capital of Ohio, has a feeling toward the Negroes all its own. In all my travels in the state I found nothing just like it."[16] It was not, Quinlan suggested, so much a rabid feeling of prejudice against Negroes simply because their skin was black, as it was a bitter hatred for them because they were what they were, character and habits. "The Negroes are almost completely outside the pale of the white people's sympathy in this city," Quinlan continued,"but the latter justify themselves and, in fact, many of the better class Negroes agree with them, on the ground that so many of the Negroes are proving themselves by their attitude and conduct unworthy of the respect of decent people. This condition of affairs has been growing by leaps and bounds during the last five or ten years. Most of the colored people say that it is only since the coming of a large number of disreputable southern Negroes that affairs have grown worse. The white people seem to think that the late-comers are prone to assert 'their rights' a little too freely. Whatever the cause may be, this much is evident--the feeling against the Negroes is bitter in the extreme."[17]

These attitudes and opinions by even so-called liberal whites haunted Allen. World War I had brought many southern Blacks northward seeking employment. To help them, in 1917, while still Executive Secretary of the Spring Street YMCA, he organized the Columbus Urban League. Gradually he formed the opinion he could better serve Black people through the Urban League than through the YMCA, and in 1921 he severed his relationship with the "Y" and formally assumed full-time duties as Executive Secretary of the Columbus Urban League.

Now Allen's unusual abilities were more fully unleashed. Through him, the door that barred blacks from the Columbus, Ohio, Labor market was finally forced open. He organized the "Friendly Service Bureau" under the police department to combat a growing crime wave. The program, recognized as the first crime prevention program in the United States, was studied and adopted by some ninety cities from coast to coast. Other national contributions made by the Columbus Urban League under Nimrod Allen's guidance were: (1) First to introduce a program to promote inter-racial goodwill as a basis for Urban League work. (2) First to introduce membership as a vehicle to spread the League'sprogram of education (later adopted throughout the League movement). (3) First to coordinate the press, radio, police department, and responsible citizens working together in the interest of promoting interracial harmony. He developed an Urban League program to execute the plan through four departments: public relations, industrial, youth and community, and neighborhood. A typical example of some of the methods used to bring about harmony between races was the "on-the-spot adjustment campaign," which was conducted annually by the public relations department.

Through Mr. Allen's vision his "Columbus Plan" in later years brought favorable national recognition to Columbus when the city was selected as one of the top ten cities in the United States for its good interracial relations. An important ingredient in creating this atmosphere was Nimrod Allen's weekly interpretations of interracial attitudes for twelve years over radio stations WBNS and WHKC. The program, entitled "The Lighthouse" featured Black men of renown, like Ralph J. Bunche, a founder and key diplomat of the United Nations. Later, when television entered the picture, "The Lighthouse" was switched to station WTVN.

Wherever he went in his travels around the country, Allen looked for examples of Black men performing valuable service or providing leadership to fellow Blacks. When he uncovered a case, he would publicize it in Opportunity or Crisis Magazine (the publications issued by the Urban League and the NAACP, respectively) or in the Black newspapers, or in his public addresses or radio programs.[18]

Other activities of Nimrod Allen included: membership in Alpha Phi Alpha Fraternity, Masonics, Elks, Knights of Pythias, Businessmen's Clubs, etc. He was president of the Ohio Conference of Social Workers Among Negroes, and he founded the Big Walnut Country Club of Columbus. He organized the Columbus Industrial Mortgage Company and the Clarod

Service Company, a brokerage Company, and he was Manager-Owner of Allen Enterprises in Columbus. His influence was felt in the organizing of business and religious ventures which acquired national importance.

In 1951 the Columbus Citizen, a Scripps-Howard newspaper, named him one of the "Ten Men of the Year" who had contributed most to Columbus. Nimrod Allen's retirement from the Urban League in June 1954, after thirty-three years of service, was headlined in Ohio's leading newspaper in Black newspapers throughout the country.

"The only aspiration I have ever had to be an expert on anything was to be one on organizations," said Allen. "I developed this theory: Organizing a group is like baking a cake. The success of it depends upon the proper ingredients, the skill of the mixing, and temperature of the oven. That to live, an organization must serve. One that is based only on selfishness will soon die. I never became an expert on organizations, but I have been blessed in having been given the opportunity to work with and through them."[19]

Although Joseph S. Himes, Jr., in his brief history, states that only six men formed the core group of the Frontiers movement, Nimrod Allen, himself, lists nine men asorganizers of the temporary organization. They were: N. B. Allen, John P. Bowles, J. S. Himes, Jr., F. F. Whittaker, Orval E. Peyton, Bruce Johnson, L. M. Shaw, C. W. Warfield, and Dr. J. J. Carter.

"Few persons," said Allen, "who have had to build from an idea escape some rough experiences and situations. One's strength is tested frequently. There are certain elements like: selfishness, jealousy, ignorance, and standpatism (complacency) that the organizers have to constantly face in trying to get an organization into orbit, especially when no selfish gains are in the offing. On the other hand, there were those few unselfish persons who formed the leaven in the movement, from whose efforts and sacrifices progress was made."[20]

7

NOTES

[1]Joseph S. Himes, Jr., "The Frontiers Movement," Opportunity, vol. 20, August 1942, p. 232.

[2]Ibid.

[3]Ibid.

[4]Ibid.

[5]Ibid., p. 233.

[6]Ibid., p. 234.

[7]F. A. Johnson, "In Memoriam," 37th Convention of Frontiers International, Springfield, Ill., July 16-21, 1978.

[8]Nimrod B. Allen, "A Brief of Human Interest Stories About Nimrod B. Allen," undated, a personal statement.

[9]Ibid.

[10]Ibid.

[11]Ibid.

[12]Ibid.

[13]A. L. Foster, "The Spring Street Branch YMCA of Columbus, Ohio," The Competitor, vol. II, Issue 1, pp. 9-12.

[14]Ibid.

[15]Ibid.

[16]Nimrod B. Allen, "East Long Street," Crisis; A Record of The Darker Races, vol. 24, November 1922, p. 12.

[17]Ibid., pp. 12-13.

8

[18]Nimrod B. Allen, "Doing His Bit," <u>Opportunity</u>, vol. 4, December 1926, pp. 385-386.

[19]Allen, op. cit., "A Brief of Human. . ."

[20]Nimrod B. Allen, "The Finders," A statement written to his wife Clara Wilson Allen, undated, p. l.

CHAPTER II

HAROLD L. PILGRIM

There was one who was neither a charter member nor an International President whose ideas and personality made so great an impact upon the growth and direction of the organization that no history of Frontiers International which omitted mention of him could possibly be considered complete. This man was Yokefellow Harold L. Pilgrim, who served as the organization's Executive Secretary for 18 years, from 1959 to 1977. Although he and Nimrod Allen were contemporaries, the men did not meet until both were more than 50 years of age. Once having met, however, the bond between them became inseparable.

Frontiers faced many problems during that period of intense civil rights struggle, and the Executive Secretary's Annual Reports chronicled them in his precise and eloquent language. In 1974 he began his written Annual Report as follows:

> Greetings: For the 15th year but one I have had
> the honor of greeting you as your Executive
> Secretary. From the creation of Frontiers
> International to the present we have been
> honorably served by 15 Presidents, including our
> current one, and I have had the pleasure of
> working with ten of them. . . During the past
> years we have been faced with uncontrollable
> competition in many areas; as rapidly as we
> recruited members of respectable standing, they
> have been siphoned off by other service organ-
> izations who have been unwilling to seek them
> out, train, and put them to work servicing their
> communities. That has been one of the reasons
> why our growth may have been somewhat stunted.

> It is, therefore, evident that we need field
> leaders whose intestinal fortitude must be
> without question, and who will be willing to
> face any area problems in the hope of winning

and keeping the confidence of those we have succeeded in securing, in order that we may be able to hold and expand their loyalty to Frontiers.

To those who have maintained their active participation and have not wavered no matter how difficult problems may have appeared to be, we must, without question, extend our highest appreciation for their continued loyalty.

Harold Latrob Pilgrim, Sr., was born in Barbados, West Indies, May 16, 1892. Upon graduating from one of the Island's private boys' schools, where cultural studies and vocational trades were taught, he worked for a few years as a tailor. In 1911 he left Barbados and came to New York City, and from that time the United States became his permanent home.

From 1917 to 1919 (World War I), Pilgrim served in the United States Army with the combat forces in England and France and attained the rank of sergeant. In 1921 he moved to Philadelphia and entered the U. S. Postal Service as a Clerk. When he retired in 1961, he had become the first Black Superintendent of the Fairmount Station, the largest Carrier Station in the Philadelphia Division. He was hyperactive-active, studying at both Temple and Michigan State Universities, and at one time or another, serving as an International Vice-President of Frontiers, President of the Philadelphia Frontiers Club, Commander of the American Legion, President and later President Emeritus of the Afro-American Historical and Cultural Museum in Philadelphia, and Public Relations Officer for the Berean Institute of Philadelphia.

During his tenure as International Executive Secretary Pilgrim continually stressed the rulership of the International Body over any of its parts. In a March 1962 Memorandum he wrote the following:

"Many questions develop as to whether we owe preference loyalty to the parent body or the local club. . . We should all be of one mind. . . Our prime loyalty and responsibility is to the International Body, for without it none can exist as a segmentary part."

Pilgrim believed in a thoughtful selection of leadership and then the giving of complete loyalty to that leadership. He believed in making sacrifices for Frontiers and spoke of the sacrifice as an "investment in the future" and he, himself, was willing to "go anywhere, meet with anyone, to promote the Frontiers organization."

12

Through Pilgrim's strong advocacy the widely scattered, jealously autonomous clubs were linked into definable regions (later districts), and active club work became a twelve-month rather than a six-month operation. In his Annual Report of 1961 he wrote: "Legislation will be suggested which will attempt to remove this organization from an operational area of six months (January to June), to a year-round going business."

On fiscal matters, in his Annual Report of 1973, Pilgrim wrote: "You are here to evaluate the activities of Frontiers in finance, membership, and all other areas. . . For that reason my responsibility is to call your attention, as graphically as possible, to statistical information, facts molded into figures. With that in your possession you, yourselves, will be in a position to develop all necessary answers."

The words and deeds of the Founder, Nimrod Allen, inspired Pilgrim, and he was determined to make Frontiers International a vital addition to American society. In addition, his distinguished services as a prominent Protestant Episcopal Churchman of the Diocese of Pennsylvania, President of the 1976 Bi-Centennial Corporation of Pennsylvania, President Emeritus of the Afro-American Historical and Cultural Museum and numerous other civic groups, attests to the dedication of his life of service to the community. A big man, with broad features that could have served as a model for the Egyptian Sphinx, his dignified bearing and scholarly address lent overwhelming weight to his message, so that his own philosophy, as well as Allen's, was indelibly stamped upon the character and course of the Fronti ers International.

CHAPTER III

YEARS OF GROWTH

J. S. Himes, Jr., of Columbus, Ohio, wrote the first constitution for Frontiers. J. Harvey Kerns of Cincinnati, Ohio, drafted the original outline from which the first Frontiers Manual was written. The "Ice Breaker" and closing hymns were written by Walter Henry of the Salem, New Jersey, Chapter, and Samuel R. Shepard was the first person to be elected editor of the anticipated Frontiersman Newsletter. However, the first national recorded publishing of the Frontiersman appears to be in March of 1962 under the editorship of W. Anthony Gaines at Delaware State College, Dover, Delaware.[1]

It was necessary, in order to get the movement before the public as a national organization, to break the bounds of Ohio and get into the movement some large industrial cities.

"The first city," said Allen, "that I visited outside Ohio was Baltimore, Maryland; I had written my colleague, Edward D. Lewis, asking his cooperation in setting up a Frontiers Club. He was, then, Executive Secretary of the Baltimore Urban League."[2]

On February 10, 1942, Allen called together a luncheon, at his own expense, in the YMCA. A group of business and professional men who, after listening to him and upon Yokefellow Lewis's recommendation, formed the first temporary Frontiers Club outside the State of Ohio.

One day later, February 11th, Allen met with a group of business and professional men in Philadelphia.

"I felt," Allen suggested, "that the attitude was 'what can this little man from the small town of Columbus, Ohio, have to offer the great city of Philadelphia?'"[3]

15

As Allen endeavored to sell the Frontiers Club idea, it appeared that the men were "throwing the book at him" in posing hypothetical problems. Time was running out as he had to catch a train back to Columbus, when Yokefellow Ervin Underhill turned the tide. "Fellows," he said, "this man is touched! Let's go along with him!" So great was the impact of this statement that a temporary organization was formed immediately, and the beginning of the Frontiers was becoming a reality.

The Eastern Organizer, Yokefellow Sparks, accompanied Allen to the railroad station, and they were both exuberant because with the Baltimore experience of the day before fresh in their minds, they realized that now Frontiers had gone into orbit as a national organization.[4]

"There had been sadness," continued Allen, "throughout the small group of Frontiersmen in Ohio when Henry C. (Hank) Sparks left Akron, where he was a charter member of the club, to assume a position with the Christian Street YMCA of Philadelphia, but it turned out to be one of the greatest of blessings to the organization."

On February 19, 1942, Baltimore, and on February 20, 1942, Philadelphia, formally entered the family of the Frontiers of America.

The next significant occurrence for Frontiers was when the opportunity came to extend its boundaries into the South. Up to then, Midwest and East were the only sections in the movement. The following news release on November 13, 1944, tells the story. It pinpoints how J. Rupert Picott and William M. Cooper became important members of the Frontiers Organization:

> The Frontiers of America was accepted and
> recommended by the Business and Professional
> Men's Conference which convened at Hampton
> Institute, Virginia, November 1 and 2, 1944, as
> the organization whose blueprint should be
> accepted by all communities where there is need
> to develop Negro leadership and support liberal
> and progressive movements and organizations.[5]
>
> N. B. Allen, Founder and National President of
> Frontiers of America, and Executive Secretary of
> the Columbus Urban League, delivered the main
> speech at the Conference banquet. He pointed
> out that the need of trained, informed, intel-

ligent, and sincere leadership is the primary
need of the Negro today, and it is also the
objective of the Frontiers of America to develop
that kind of leadership.[6]

The Conference Call was issued by NEWHAMPS, an
organization of the business and professional
men of the Virginia Peninsula, which included
the cities of Newport News and Hampton, and by
the EXTENSION DIVISION OF HAMPTON INSTITUTE.
J. Rupert Picott is Secretary of NEWHAMPS and
William M. Cooper is Director of the EXTENSION
DIVISION AT HAMPTON INSTITUTE. The Conference
Call was sent out because it was recognized
that there is a need for a coming together of
representatives of the various business and
professional organizations located throughout
our country for the purpose of forming a
national organization through which projects,
ideas, and information of mutual concern to all
such clubs and groups can be cleared and
disseminated.

Resolutions passed were:

　　1. That we recognize the great worth of
our existing organizations and wish in no wise
to duplicate the important work they are doing.

　　2. That we approve the service club idea
such as exemplified by the Rotary, Kiwanis, and
Lions Internationals but recognize special
adjustments must be made to meet the peculiar
needs of the Negro as a minority group. Outstanding among these peculiar needs is the need
for a sincere informed diversified leadership
selected by and developed within the ranks of
our own people.

　　3. That through the fellowship provided in
the service clubs it will be possible to dis-
cover and develop the leadership referred to
above.

4. That, further, we recognize the importance of groups to support liberals and progressive movements and organizations in each respective community.

5. That we recognize in the Frontiers of America a national organization whose blueprint developed through the past seven years embodies the principles set forth above. For this reason, we commend this organization to all communities where such services are needed.[7]

The headquarters for the Frontiers of America was at 107 North Monroe Avenue, Columbus, Ohio. Mr. Nimrod Allen was national president, and L. M. Shaw was national secretary.

Members of the Resolutions Committee were: Rev. M. J. Sherad, President, Civic and Professional Club, Augusta, Georgia; Rev. O. J. Hawkins, Assistant Secretary, Negro Civic Club, Wilson, North Carolina; Nimrod B. Allen, President, Frontiers of America, Columbus, Ohio; William R. Walker, Jr., President, Newhamps, Hampton, Virginia; George W. Cox, Vice-President, North Carolina Mutual Life Insurance Company; and William M. Cooper, Hampton Institute, Chairman.[8]

Yokefellow Cooper became Southern Organizer from 1945 through 1949. During that time he brought into the Frontiers movement the following clubs: Newhamp and Norfolk, Virginia; Charleston and Florence, South Carolina; and he rendered service in bringing Omaha, Nebraska into the movement.

Yokefellow Picott was the sparkplug of this assembly at Hampton Institute and gave valuable encouragement to the acceptance by this group of the Frontiers movement.[9]

One of the myths accentuated by those persons who had little faith in the accomplishments of Black men in American life was easily dispelled by men who joined and were active in the Frontiers International.

The "Frontiers of America" as it was incorporated in the State of Ohio on December 24, 1938, became "Frontiers Internation" (changed to "International" in 1962). "Frontiers International Incorporated" became the full title and also became another vehicle to help the promise of social progress for Blacks in America. In that same year (i.e. 1962) a club charter was granted to a club in British Guiana.

Serving as image bearers for young Black males "The Frontiers, historically, has been made up of Black men functioning at local club levels. Men from the business, educational, and professional worlds represented the foci of membership. They tended to have a strong commitment to service and a sense for a better way of life for the less fortunate."[10] Community consciousness and a dedicated spirit of humanity have found many of the Frontiers membership (including the Frontiers Women's Auxiliary) active in organizations like the YMCA and YWCA, the United Way, the NAACP, the Urban League, various fraternities and sororities, and the Big Brother and Big Sister programs.

The strength of the Frontiers International, since its inception, has been the programming and activities of its local clubs. It was born out of a period of change and turmoil in the 1930's. America was hit with a lethal case of economic depression. In the midst of incessant and nagging social difficulties, the Frontiers "managed to maintain a posture of service to the deprived and needy in the minority community."[11]

Support for college scholarships, blood donations, finding jobs for the needy, serving as Big Brothers to youngsters without fathers at home, donating materials to Black college libraries, and providing food for the hungry, were merely a few activities implemented by the organization during those years.

One of the major projects undertaken by the Frontiers in 1950 was the establishment of the first and only national foundation dedicated exclusively to the provision of funds for the research, treatment, and cure of Vitiligo (a disease which robs its victims of skin color).

In each community where a Frontiers chapter existed, special needs accentuated special responses. A college-bound project in one community might have been supplanted by a blood donation drive in another community. The Frontiers-men were always present to respond and give service to those in need.

Some clubs throughout the country were fortunate enough to establish auxiliary clubs (made up of the wives and daughters of active or deceased members of the Frontiers). With the support of women many programs and activities became successful. Innovative insights and projected goals were easily clarified and carried out with their support.

After future goals and insights were envisioned by the founder, Nimrod B. Allen, and his cohorts, in 1936, a central aim of the Frontiers movement came into focus: "the discovery, stimulation, and development of effective and untrammeled leaders for unselfish community service."[12]

Over a period of time as many Frontiersmen met in their club activities, there emerged an umbrella posture of group solidarity and loyalty to principles of community service. Club activity, as a result, drew community leaders together. It gave them an opportunity to exchange views and ideas, "pick up valuable current information. . . and to agree on fundamental objectives and techniques for service and club growth. It is important to note that the motivating factors and stimulants which led to direct action were: "Frontiers Club members sought opportunities to service existing organizations (e.g. as members and officers of boards, committees, fund and membership campaigns, etc.). The other pattern taken by service-motivated and inspired Frontiers leaders has been an alertness to meet the unmet needs of a community."[13]

Between February 1939 and July 1939, the formation and chartering of the Frontiers Clubs of Columbus, Akron, and Cincinnati, Ohio, were in place, followed shortly by clubs organized in Dayton, Ohio, Baltimore, Maryland and Philadelphia Pennsylvania, and the experiment to spread the organization and its mission began to work. In a historical statement published by Ebony Magazine in January 1962, the author, William A. Boone, suggested that the "Frontiers was the only Black service organization in America (on the order of Rotary, Lions, and Kiwanis Clubs) which met the many needs of the minority community in service.

Another significant statement appeared in a 1969 Ebony article:

Independent in action and free of political
affiliation, Frontiers International, Inc.,
attracts some of the most substantial and
well-educated residents of the Negro community.
Members, however, are quick to point out that
they are "not snobbish." Provided he is of good
character and standing in his community and is

20

engaged in an administrative capacity in a
recognized line of business, any male 21 years
of age and over may become a Frontiersman.
Although basically a Negro organization, there
are no racial restrictions.[14]

This statement, which became a policy statement of the organization, exemplified the unique character and prolific nature of how service to community life was carried out by polished men of good morals who were grandsons and great-grandsons of former slaves.

The first charter members were proud to receive the acknowledgment on December 24, 1938 (i.e. the Columbus Frontiers Club) when the State of Ohio issued the endorsement. On that day they set a precedent for a significant historical pattern throughout Black communities in America. The image of decent Black men exemplifying positive community images was exalting during a period when Adolph Hitler in Germany was vibrating messages of racism and fascism throughout the world, and U.S.A. military troops were virtually segregated.

A listing of that chartered group would be appropriate as follows:

FOUNDER, NIMROD B. ALLEN
ORGANIZERS OF TEMPORARY ORGANIZATION

N. B. Allen	Bruce Johnson
John P. Bowles	L. M. Shaw
J. S. Himes, Jr.	C. W. Warfield
F. F. Whittaker	Dr. J. J. Carter
Orval E. Peyton	

ORGANIZERS OF PERMANENT ORGANIZATION

N. B. Allen	C. W. Warfield
John P. Bowles	Charles Jones
R. M. Tribbitt	Jesse Jackson
Orval E. Peyton	L. M. Shaw
Bruce Johnson	S. D. Hooker
James W. Williams	Harrison G. Payne
F. F. Whittaker	J. S. Himes, Jr.
Dr. J. J. Carter	John R. Butler
A. P. Bentley	N. L. Scarborough

21

CHARTER MEMBERS

N. B. Allen
Talmadge Allen
Dr. John Bailey
A. P. Bentley
Elmer Burns
John R. Butler
Amos Carter
Dr. J. J. Carter
C. W. Comer
Dr. W. W. Cooper
Dr. W. H. Dyer
Z. T. Ellis
A. M. Giles
Col. H. H. Gilbert
Robert Goode
Dr. J. S. Himes, Jr.
Dr. Booker Harris
Rev. William H. Holloway
S. D. Hooker
Ray E. Hughes
Jesse Jackson
Rev. C. F. Jenkins
Bruce Johnson
Bishop R. E. Jones

Robert Jones
James Joyner
W. P. King
S. M. Lampkin
Dr. A. K. Lawrence
W. S. Lyman, Sr.
E. D. Mackey
J. Arnett Mitchell
Foster O. Newlin
Rev. Harrison G.
    Payne
Orval E. Peyton
M. B. Prince
William E. Rose
Rev. N. L.
    Scarborough
L. M. Shaw
E. D. Tate
Dr. R. M. Warfield
Rev. W. Williams
David D. White
F. F. Whittaker
J. W. Williams
Dr. H. H. Wilson

Charles W. Worley
Mrs. Mary L. Saunders
Volunteer Office Secretary-Assistant

The developing history of the Frontiers was unfolded in the activity and performance of some key individuals from the founding group. They were the spiritual backbone and the physical drivers of program achievement for the Frontiers organization.

Forest F. Whittaker, for example, was a pioneer in helping Blacks in Columbus, Ohio, who suffered from racial discrimination to become socially, spiritually, and materially sound. When Nimrod Allen called upon his help to spread the Frontiers message beyond Columbus, he was known to have furnished, at his own expense, automobiles for a caravan to other cities.

It was Leslie M. Shaw who made the motion at a meeting that the name "Frontiers" should be chosen as the organization's title. It was adopted and lives with us today. Shaw eventually became the organization's national secretary.

Dr. J. J. Carter was the first official president of the local chapter in Columbus. He served from its inception until January 1938 through 1947. It was he who conceived the idea that the Frontiers Club should take the initiative and re-establish the celebration of the Emancipation Proclamation on January 1 of each year.[16]

J. W. Williams, Sr., became the second president of the Columbus Club, serving in 1938 to January 1939. He had the honor of serving on the first Board of Directors of the National Frontiers through 1941. A staunch supporter of progress and organization, he was one of the pillars in the Frontiers who helped the program get beyond its infancy stage.

J. S. Himes, Jr., was Research Director of the Columbus Urban League. As secretary of the local Club he wrote the constitution and kept the early minutes for the organization. He served in this capacity from 1939 to 1943. As an organizer and charter member of Frontiers, he helped to "spread the word" on trips to other states which were taken with the hope of establishing new Frontiers Clubs.[17]

It was George W. Thompson who was singularly responsible for Akron, Ohio being the second city to affiliate in the movement. He made the initial contacts and "set up the meetings for representatives of the Columbus Club to talk with representative citizens of Akron." He also made a noteworthy contribution "in using the facilities of the Akron Community Center to promote the Frontiers Club of the city."[18]

James A. Maddox, a distinguished citizen of Columbus, worked with the Chamber of Commerce and was the sparkplug for civic and social affairs, especially fund-raising campaigns. He tended to be the "booster for all good causes." He had the privilege of installing the first officers of the Columbus Club in 1937 on a Sunday morning at the Second Baptist Church of Columbus.

M. F. Bratcher held the distinction of holding the office of secretary of a local club longer than any other Frontiersman. He was also one of the organizers of the Akron, Ohio chapter.

A stalwart in the Frontiers movement was Artee Fleming. He became the first president of the Akron Club. He also held the honor of becoming a member and chairman of the National Board of Directors of Frontiers from

1938 to 1949. He then took on the responsibility of National Secretary from 1949 to 1952.[19]

It was J. Harvey Kerns who pioneered the establishment of the third Frontiers Club in Cincinnati, Ohio. In his professional area he was a great contributor to community life as Director of the Division of Negro Welfare in Cincinnati. Yokefellow Kerns was chairman of the committee to write the first manual of the Frontiers. He drafted the original outline from which the manual was written. He also served on the National Board of Directors for Frontiers from 1939 to 1944.

Henry C. (Hank) Sparks became Eastern Organizer in 1940. He served as third vice-president from 1939 to 1942, and from 1942 to 1943 he served another term as third vice-president. Beginning in 1940 through 1962 he served as Eastern Organizer. Finally, he served as second vice-president in 1945 to 1946 for the National Frontiers movement. During this time his influence was felt not only in the East but anywhere there was a possibility of organizing a Frontiers Club. Said Nimrod Allen: "The great growth of the Frontiers of America in the East is due largely to his impact, energy, and foresight."[20]

Ervin W. Underhill was the first president of the Frontiers Club in Philadelphia. In 1942 he was elected to the membership of the Board of Directors and served from 1942 to 1943.

A group of important Frontiers historical figures followed who were the impetus of a national effort to make the Frontiers International, Inc., a viable program on the national scene. They were: Robert R. Neal (Board of Director for the National, 1941; member of the Akron Club; Midwestern Organizer, 1946-48; National Secretary, 1948; helped to organize the Cincinnati Chapter; organized the chapter in Marion, Indiana, under the direction of Joseph Casey, first president, in 1943; participated in the organization of the Pittsburgh, Pennsylvania, the Chicago and Rockford, Illinois, Clubs). Wayne L. Hopkins (a strong Philadelphia Club supporter; contact person with the national office and Eastern Organizer; member of the Board of Directors of the National Frontiers from 1948 to 1949 and 1954 to 1955;) Walter T. Henry (organizer of the Salem, New Jersey Club and was its first president; elected third vice-president of the National Organization in 1946 to 1948); Earl E. Campbell (organized the Dayton, Ohio club in July 1941, which was the last of the four Ohio Clubs that formed the nucleus that made the organization national); J. Arnett Mitchell (a charter member of the Columbus Club; member of the Board of Directors 1944 to 1945 and 1958 to 1959; member of the committee on writing the first Frontiers Manual, which was composed of Harvey Kerns, chairman, N. B. Allen, and J. S. Himes,

Jr.); L. F. Palmer (played a major role in the historic 1946 convention which recognized the Frontiers as an official nationalized organization); W. T. Nelson (first president and organizer of the Frontiers Club in Cincinnati, Ohio; a pioneer in the YMCA, Division of Negro Welfare, Council of Social Agencies Department, and the Community Chest of Cincinnati and Hamilton County; First Vice-President of National from 1939 through 1946); Mary L.Saunders (Even though a woman and not eligible, during the early years due to membership requirements, she held the position as clerk-stenographer for Frontiers. She traveled to conventions, board meetings, etc. She was the first woman to be cited by the organization for service rendered to the Frontiers movement); John L. Berry and Alexander J. Allen (Berry, first vice-president and Allen, first secretary of the Baltimore Chapter, were instrumental in getting the Baltimore Club program in motion); W. W. Cooper (was the fourth president of the Columbus Frontiers); C. M. Cain (organizer of the Atlantic City, New Jersey Club on February 19, 1944; served as chairman of the Board of Directors from 1950 to 1959; hosted two Frontiers conventions in Atlantic City, 1947 and 1950); and Samuel R. Shepard (became the first person to be elected editor of the anticipated Frontiersman, and served as Sergeant-at-arms for national conventions from 1939 through 1946).[21]

In a brief historical statement printed in the 1962 edition of Ebony Magazine, William A. Boone was quoted as saying ". . . the Frontiers, the only Negro service organization in America (on the order of Rotary and Kiwanis Clubs), has gone far beyond its initial task of assisting only Negroes. In each of the 73 communities in the 27 states where Frontiers has charters, the entire community has profited, both materially and socially, as a result of the selfless leadership of the now 3,500-member strong organization formed for only one purpose: to serve." The article further emphasized the key to how the Frontiers Clubs function in their various communities throughout the country, and how the energy, concern, and participation in and for community growth has been undertaken by serious Black male business and professional visionaries:

> The service may be small gestures, like buying a
> graduation dress for a financially poor student,
> or planting a tree on the grounds of a revered
> institution. The service may be large in scope,
> like the Frontiers $10,000 grant for research
> and cure of vitiligo, a dreaded disease causing
> loss of pigment in the skin which affects one in
> every ten persons in America. The service may
> be constant, like the annual presentations of
> scholarships and awards of recognition to worthy

individuals or groups. Or, the service may be
unusual, like supplying seeing eye dogs for the
blind. But whether the act is large or small,
it is an example of the Frontiersmen's dedication to a purpose which is embodied in their
national motto--ADVANCEMENT THROUGH SERVICE.[22]

As the oldest Black male service organization in the United States,
Frontiers International holds a unique position. Its history, like those of the
National Association for the Advancement of Colored People (NAACP) and
the National Urban League, forms a spoke in the wheel that links the past
and present in the lives of Black Americans. Like the NAACP and Urban
League, Frontiers established a network of individuals and clubs across the
United States of America. Unlike them, Frontiers' main thrust was not
political or economic, but was and still is, to render unselfish community
service.

Most Frontiers Clubs have been formed in the inner cities, and
although much of their membership no longer live there, the problems they
attempt to solve are the problems of the urban inner cities. Through the
turbulent end of the Depression-plagued 1930s, Frontiers managed to maintain
a posture of service to the deprived and needy in the Black community.
Activities like support for college scholarships, giving blood, finding jobs for
the needy, serving as Big Brothers, donating reading materials to Black
college libraries, and providing food for the hungry were just a few of the
activities endorsed by those early chartered Frontiers Clubs.

Nimrod B. Allen, the Founder, set a strong pace from Columbus, Ohio,
in 1936. Prior to the Second World War years, every step of progress taken
by Black Americans was a step into a new frontier. Allen and his subsequent
proteges made the Frontiers program work by dedicating their lives to its
premise. Their efforts tended to eradicate the notion of Black male
inferiority and Black male limitations. In short, Frontiers projects the image
of a Black male rescue squad that offers a hand to those, particularly of
minority groups, who are destitute of hope.

The Frontiersman's only outward display of membership in the
organization is a half-inch diameter blue and gold pin worn in his coat lapel.
Its members, however, share several common bonds. One bond is that they
have all been relatively successful in life despite the prejudiced treatment
administered to Black males by the majority society. Another bond is that its
members are dedicated to service, to giving, without expecting anything in
return. A third bond is that nearly all of them are civic leaders in their local
communities. They are the chairmen, co-chairmen, or active members of the

Boards of the YMCA, the Boy Scouts, the School, the Neighborhood House, the United Way, the Urban League, the NAACP, etc.

Since the work of Frontiers has become, to a great extent, standardized, the combination of many clubs working on a few International objectives makes the Frontiers a strong national factor in addition to its strong local influence in those cities where clubs exist.

A powerful cementing factor for the organization is its annual Convention. With only a few exceptions, over its fifty-odd years of history, the Conventions have been held during the month of July, and from 1982 to date (1990) each Convention has started on Wednesday and ended on Saturday night, with the Board of Directors settling all unfinished business at a Sunday morning session, a total period of four and one-half days. Care is taken that consecutive Convention sites are selected in different regions of the country to avoid creating any continuity of travel hardships for any of the seven active districts of clubs.[23]

The first Convention was held October 15, 1939 in Columbus, Ohio, at Nimrod Allen's own Monroe Avenue Social Center, as was the second, which was held July 27 to 29 in 1940. The next twenty years, excluding 1943, 44 and 45 when the Conventions were suspended, all Conventions were held at Black-owned or operated institutions.

Several years before the passage of the 1964 Civil Rights bill, the Frontiers began probing the discrimination barriers. In 1961 the Convention was held at the Sheraton Hotel in Akron, Ohio; in 1962 at the Sheraton in Philadelphia; and in 1963 at the Sheraton-Blackstone in Chicago. After the 1964 bill was passed Frontiers celebrated by holding its 1965 Convention at the Waldorf Astoria Hotel in New York City.

For most Frontiersmen the Convention became a yearly trek to a moveable shrine. In those four and one-half days there occurred a major election of officers, a banquet, two major luncheons, a convention photograph, a memorial service, a "get-acquainted party," several major workshops, awards, extensive committee assignments for delegates, a look anew at the organization's Constitution and By-Laws, and, for accompanying families a chance to tour, or play, through the courtesy of the host club.

The Women's Auxiliary, known as the Coordinating Council, met at the same time and location but conducted separate business meetings. The two groups combined for the President's Banquet, the Vitiligo Symposium, and the Memorial Service. The luncheons were optional.

27

Many clubs came to the Conventions with club banners and brochures. Many set up booths which showed historical pictures of the past year's activities. All District Directors set up suites which served as the Convention base for the clubs in their Districts.

From the "Get Acquainted" party on Wednesday evening to Saturday evening's closing banquet, the Convention moved at a furious pace. Every year's election process generated its own excitement, but since the International President normally served only two years and was usually succeeded by the First Vice-President, the upward succession of Vice-Presidents left a vacancy at the Third Vice-President position every other year which created an intensive lobby between the seven Districts. No District, by itself, was strong enough to elect an International Officer, and so the lobbying to gain the support of other Districts consisted of bargaining, persuasion, compromise, and future commitments to return the favor. In fact, the strategy to be applied in presenting resolutions and nominees began at the District workshops and conferences.

Added to the electioneering lobby was the lobby created by Clubs which wanted their cities as future Convention sites, and the lobbies created by individuals who were crusaders for a cause not on the established agenda.

The Convention afforded a panoramic vision of the Frontiers International at work and play. Here, at work, the national agenda of Black pride was promulgated, and there, at play, were the vendors selling products as varied as fruit cakes and T-shirts. Here, at work, were the members who were anxious to get a critical appraisal of their National Officers, and there, at play, were the Yokefellows and Yokettes who came for the social side and nothing more. In the end, however, it was from here, through the efforts of the International Officers, the Committee Reports, and the exchanged stories of local heroics, that the delegates were inspired to return home as "born again" disciples of the Frontiers philosophy: "Advancement through Service."

After several years of decline Frontiers began to grow again. Its decline was largely due to active solicitation of Black members by formerly all-white service clubs and the lack of effort by Frontiers to compete for new Black members. Black male professional and businessmen, once excluded from Kiwanis, Lions, Optimists and Rotary Clubs, were now sought as avidly as Black athletes were in professional sports. Like the old Negro Baseball League, Frontiers found its ranks decimated by aggressive competition.

However, service-oriented Black professionals were turning or returning to Frontiers as they discovered that the greatest help they could render young ghetto Blacks was the sight of successful Black men working among them in their interest through an organization founded and controlled by Blacks.

Every Frontiers Club had a unique story to tell about its contributions to community life and development. The Nashville, Tennessee Club, for example, had many of their activities published in the local paper, The Tennessean: "Frontiers International Sets New Youth Program" (May 20, 1968); "Dr. Crouch Gets World Post" a Yokefellow (August 7, 1968); "Peppery Sara Adds First To Frontiers Convention" -- referring to Sara Dickerson, International President of the Auxiliary of Frontiers (July 25, 1977); "Frontiers Join Tabloid Sale" -- referring to helping sell the Junior League Home for Crippled Children's Palm Sunday Tabloid (February 10, 1971); "Whitney Young Speech slated for March 27" -- Young was Executive Director of the National Urban League (March 1968); and "Frontiers Club To Stress Stronger Ties With Youth" (July 30, 1967).[24]

Another example was the Milwaukee Club, founded by Peter Murrell and Thomas Cheek in 1955, with a membership of 18 men. They were involved in local Milwaukee activities like: the Little Buddy Program; vocational guidance clinics for high school students; membership campaigns for the YMCA, and other youth support programs. Encouraged by members of the National Frontiers Board, who felt that Milwaukee was fertile territory for the formation of a new Frontiers Club, their intuition became a reality. Yokefellow Thomas Cheek attended the Annual Convention held in Chicago in August 1955 to gather information from the many delegates from other chapters. Cheek and Murrell were able to convince eighteen men of the social significance of the Frontiers' program. As a result, these men (i.e., five attorneys, two doctors, one dentist, two teachers, two probation officers, one engineer, one businessman, a YMCA executive, a city alderman, the Director of the Urban League, and two professional city employees in public relations) held their first meeting in September 1955, elected Peter Murrell to chair the meeting, formed a nominating committee, and put together their new officers:

President   - Peter Murrell
Vice-President   - Thomas Cheek
Secretary   - William J. Carr
Treasurer   - Roy Wilson.

The new slate of officers were officially installed at a charter banquet (held at Hubbard Lodge) on January 18, 1956. The charter was presented by Frontiers founder, Nimrod Allen, and a gateway of concerned citizens who planned to help the needy of Milwaukee was opened.

29

Early efforts to help the youth of Milwaukee led to the establishment of a Little Buddy Program (a program similar to Big Brother, i.e., becoming a companion to a boy in need by exposing him to activities not experienced previously).

Other activities which kept Milwaukee Yokefellows busy were: an annual Founder's Day Program; bimonthly Sunday afternoon forums (an outstanding young man, Vel Phillips, the first Black native-born Milwaukean to graduate from a local high school, became a lawyer and a local leader; and the first woman and only Black to be elected Secretary of the State of Wisconsin, served on the forum panel); golf tournaments to raise funds for needy; and supported day care centers.

In 1979 the Milwaukee Club was awarded the Human Rights Award by B'Nai B'Rith, giving recognition to their concern for community development and meeting the needs of those who call out for help.[25]

The Tallahassee Club, organized on September 20, 1953. They have been very active in community project services, for example: School Boy Patrol (a survival program); Little Buddy Project (a Big Brother concept); Annual Awards (for achievement); Volunteer Services to Headstart (a government support program for economically deprived children); Looking Ahead Project (a training session for graduating high school seniors); substantial monetary awards; and Special Project Efforts and vitiligo research.[26]

The Annapolis, Maryland Club, organized in 1947. Involved in a number of meaningful projects exemplifying the motto: "Advancement Through Service." Some of the activities were: Sponsored a patient at the Howard University Vitiligo Clinic; Provided financial assistance for renovating the Parole Health Center; gave financial assistance to the Arundel General Hospital, the Anne Arundel County Fine Arts Festival Show, the AA County General Hospital blood bank project, and life membership to the NAACP; provided counseling service for parents with disruptive children; sponsored a scout troop; visitations to community church services; visited penal institutions and presented programs; and supported many other local community activities related to equal opportunity and community cooperation.[27]

Dedicated service came through the efforts of the Plainfield Area Club of New Jersey, organized September 14, 1961. It had diligently, over the years, tried to live up to the ideals and principles of the Frontiers movement. Some of its activities were: Sponsored in 1961 Boy Scout Troop No. 6; published a local Frontiers Bulletin; helped to create the Plainfield Human Relations Committee's Tutoring service for needy students; Offered Plainfield its first Black representatives in public affairs in the persons of Yokefellows Dr. James H. Reid as a City Councilman, and Dr. Richard F. Neblett on the Board of Education; donated funds to the Neighborhood House and the YMCA, etc.; sponsored the Dr. Martin Luther King Breakfast as an annual affair; and supported the Big Brother program.

In the 1963 program for the Frontiers International Convention, the pamphlet highlighted the Frederick, Maryland chapter. The club listed its accomplishments from 1954 to 1963. In 1954 the club became involved in the issue of housing for the needy; in 1955 it hosted the 12-year old national spelling champion, Gloria Lockerman; and it also, in that same year, financially aided in the purchase of the city's first ambulance. The chapter became the first Black group to be registered with the local Chamber of Commerce, "which holds the first Charter granted in the U. S."[28] In 1957 an annual Frontier Cotillion began. Many local high school coeds benefited each year. In that same year the Club took out a life membership in the NAACP. The highlight of 1958 was the presentation of Secretary Richard Maximillan Okwei of the "New" Republic of Ghana at a special meeting of all heads of civic and service organizations of Frederick, Maryland.[29] In 1959 a revolving educational scholarship plan was initiated. A number of students benefited. Also, a $2,000 gift was awarded to the Frederick Memorial Hospital Building Fund, which assured the chapter a memorial room in the hospital.[30] In 1960 buses were provided to transport local citizens, free of charge, to be present at a session of the State Legislature of Maryland which dealt with the subject of Public Accommodations. And in 1963 the Club pledged $500 to the new YMCA Building Fund, which was put on an enscribed mosaic in the lobby in the section reserved for Service Clubs.[31]

In the 1963 pamphlet on the Frontiers Convention the Baton Rouge Frontiers Club, Louisiana listed in its membership: Yokefellows Hezekiah Jackson; Charles R. Evans; C. J. Gilliam; Vanderbilt Sewell; S. J. Ramsey; Theodore J. Jamison; Raymond P. Scott; L. L. Haynes, Jr., John Williams; John G. Lewis; Joseph M. Dyer; W. T. Hanley, Jr.; J. L. Kraft; Homer J. Sheeler; G. Leon Netterville, Jr.; R. V. Simms; and Johnnie A. Jones. This chapter's leadership in the community of Baton Rouge, Louisiana reactivated the local chapter of the NAACP; conducted a parish-wide voter registration campaign; and was generally involved in local institutional issues--educational, correctional, vocational and business.[32]

Listed also in the 1963 pamphlet was the Chicago Club with fourteen charter members: William R. Hammond, president; William P. Tuggle, Secretary; Samuel Stratton, Treasurer; G. Hamilton Martin, Chaplain; Robert L. Neal; Francis Pemberton; Arthur Turnbull; James A. Glover; William J.

White; Cecil Scott; Vernon B. Williams, Jr.; Walter J. Payne; Corneff Taylor; and Andrew "Boots" Johnson.[33] Some of their activities included Black History breakfasts; NAACP life membership; contributions to the Vitiligo Research Foundation; and financial aid to Provident Hospital, Chicago Urban League, Jane Dent Home for Aged, Randall House for Boys, Henry Horner Boys Club, Washington Park YMCA, and Boy Scouts of America.[34]

The Fort Wayne club, in 1963, outlined a very productive activity in community service which brought pride and distinction to Black men in community life. They sponsored a six-week Summer School program cooperatively with the Fort Wayne community schools--a program designed for disadvantaged and under-achieving boys and girls. One thousand fifty dollars was contributed by the club to this worthy experimental project.[35]

Other clubs listed with pride in the 1963 Convention pamphlet were Philadelphia, Newark, Vaux Hall, and New Brunswick.[36]

In the 31st Annual Convention report the Miami Club was highlighted (July 27-31, 1971): Walter Cogwell, President; Sanford Ramsey, Secretary; Elisha Hepburn; Robert Gabriel; James Cherry; G. Wendell Kitpatrick; Leroy Thompson; Royal Pugear; Oscar Weaver; Ernest Taylor; Wilbert Haynes; Alexander Brooks; and William Fuller.[37] They continued to magnify the idea of Black men dedicated to community service.

The 34th Convention, which focused on the theme, "Success is the realization of a worthwhile goal," recognized the community work of the Atlantic city Club, the Bucks Tri-County Club, the Harrisburg, Pennsylvania Club the Cleveland Club, the Kansas City Club, the Opelousas, Louisiana Club, the Delaware Club, and the Plainfield area Club.[38] Their work and achievements in community needs and services glowed as a bastion of hope for many Black Americans.

After giving recognition to the Omaha Club, the Baltimore Club, the Gary, Indiana Club, the Opelousas Club and the Philadelphia Club, the St. Louis Club submitted a little detail on their program and activity. They were proud to announce that they sponsored a youth baseball team; financially supported Vitiligo Disease Research at the Howard University Medical School; and gave ongoing financial support to the United Way.[39] The officers who helped direct the above areas of importance were: Alfred Ford, Past President; Jerome Williams, M.D., Past President; Harold Antoine, New President; J. Phillip Waring, Past President; and E. B. Koonce, Treasurer.

Carrying on the tradition, the Atlantic City Club, the Springfield Club, and small clubs like Decatur and Shelbyville were given attention in the July

1977, 36th National Convention program held in Nashville, Tennessee at the Sheraton-Nashville Hotel. They sparkled under the theme for the day, "Aiding Black Survival in Urban America Through the Frontiers Movement." A message of hope for the poor needing community support came through loud and strong, and the Frontiers organization once again took center stage.

In the July 1978 report the convention gave recognition to the Jayhawk club of Kansas City, Kansas; the Milwaukee Club; the Omaha Club; Newark Club; the Decatur Club; the Philadelphia Club; the Prince George Club; the Akron Club; and the Annapolis Club.[40] They gloried under the theme, "Black Unity Through Coordinated Services."

The Philadelphia Club stood out, in numbers and in program effort, as the National office found its home in the city of Philadelphia. In its 1978-79 Annual Report the club was proud to praise its community effort that attempted to uplift the Black populace. The activities were many. In 1978, at the new Lulu Temple in Plymouth Meeting, Pennsylvania, Count Basie and his band performed as a fund raising effort. The club netted $6,135; a strong financial commitment by the club went into changing the city charter which allowed a mayor to run for a third term and city officials to run for another office without resigning from their present position; support of Black writer and historian Mark Hyman; and strong annual financial support to the Columbia YMCA, Vitiligo Foundation, Steven Smith Geriatric Center, Philadelphia Tribune Charities; North Philadelphia Action Branch NAACP; Philadelphia Urban League; and the Philadelphia OIC (Opportunities Industrialization Center).[41]

Two clubs not consistently recognized were the North Houston Club, Texas (Henry Morgan, President; Bill Easter, Vice-President; Ray Curry, Secretary; Ed Page, Treasurer; and Anthony R. Sampson, Chaplain); and the Washington, DC Club (Charles Faunteroy, Maryland area director; and Clement Martin, Northern District Director) in the 41st Convention pamphlet held in Philadelphia, Pennsylvania, July 1982. They were complimented under the Convention theme, "Blueprint for Survival."

Nothing was more important in public life and service than the leadership provided to make an organization or group effective. The 1986 and 1987 listing of club presidents of the Frontiers was significant. A new breed of insightful Black men, some who served a number of years as Yokefellows, and others young, vigorous and energetic, all leading towards the development of a strong national profile in strong community service. In 1986 the National slate went as follows: Dale G. Lee, President; Bill Joiner, 1st Vice-President; Floyd N. Alston, 2nd Vice-President; Henry L. Morgan, Secretary; Herbert A. Wise, Treasurer; Rev. James W. Logan; George Alford,

Sergeant-at-Arms; Robert L. Johnson, Acting Administrative Director, Vitiligo Foundation, Inc.; and Guy A. Jones, Immediate Past President.[42] The National directors were: Andrew Wertz, First District; A. R. Snowden, Second District; Dr. Malcolm D. Williams, Third District; Phillip Nelson, Fourth District; A. J. Dickerson, Fifth District; Wesley L. Mitchell, Sixth District; J. D. Washington, Seventh District; Elmer Jackson, International Attorney; and Charles H. Clarke, Jr., Public Relations. The club Presidents, representing a number of states, were: Robert Earley, Akron, Ohio; Dr. Robert Threatt, Atlanta, Georgia; Fleming James, Baltimore, Maryland; Lawrence G. Cooper, Bucks County; John Mitchem, Harrisburg, Pennsylvania; Hilton Thompson, Lafayette, Louisiana; Gerald Mitchell, Mercer County; John Moutry, Milwaukee, Wisconsin; Reginald Hughes, Nashville, Tennessee; William Stubbs, Newark, New Jersey; Thomas J. Adams, Omaha, Nebraska; Wilbur Hobbs, Philadelphia, Pennsylvania; Rudolph Hampton, Springfield, Ohio; Preston Young, Stark County; James Barge, Tallahassee, Florida; Charles Stubblefield, Trenton, New Jersey; and Salomon Dennis, Washington, DC.[43] The function under the theme for that year, "Renovation '86."

The theme for the 46th Annual Convention in Milwaukee, Wisconsin, July 15-19, 1987, was reflected in the pamphlet, "Excellence In Community Service". The leadership under national officership was the same as in 1986, with exception of change in the National Treasurer; for 1987 the man who took over that post was Sinkler A. Casselle. National Directors remained the same as 1986, and club presidents added some new forces to the list: Lawrence L. Harris, Jr., Annapolis, Maryland; Rev. Willie A. Simmons, Newark, New Jersey; Dr. William H. Johnson, Omaha, Nebraska; J. J. Ewell, Opelousas, Louisiana; Que Burnell, St. Louis, Missouri; and Joe Musgray, Tallahassee, Florida.

Fifteen Black men gathered together and organized the Newark, New Jersey chapter of the Frontiers International in 1952. They were spurred on by the negative racial climate in Newark at that time, which made it difficult for responsible, community-concerned, Black men to be able to join respected white service organizations. Chartered in 1953, the new Yokefellows began to exercise their desires to help meet the pressing social and economic needs of the Black community. However, their efforts tended to benefit the entire Newark community.

According to the present president (1989) of the Newark Club, Edward L. Haynes, "The first president of the Newark Club was Attorney Virtum Bland. Under Bland's Administration, the Executive Secretary of the club was the Honorable Judge Hubert Tate. The club met every Tuesday at the Cadillac Club on Hill Street in Newark."[44]

Around 1956-57 Jim King became the president of the Newark Club. Under his leadership the club expanded its work in the community. "The club joined what was known at that time as the Civic Club Council. The Civic Club Council was made up of all the Black civic and service clubs in the city of Newark."[45]

Yokefellow James G. Eastman became a president of the Civic Club Council. Under his leadership the men involved organized into the "Mass-Organized Business and Industry" as a means of focusing on economic growth and self-help.

The Newark Club became very active in community concerns during the latter 1950's and the 1960's. For example, Yokefellow William "Bill" Ashby organized a senior citizens' picnic--an opportunity for the latter to have a day in the park and enjoy one another's company. Also, the club, during that period, "became a part of the coalition of Negro workers for the building of Negro Businesses in the City of Newark."[46]

During the decade of the 1960's the Newark Club was directly active in civil rights activities. Club President Clyde D. Mitchell, for example, joined the Rev. Martin Luther King, Jr. on the March from Selma to Montgomery, Alabama, to protest racial segregation in that state. Likewise the club sent fifteen members to participate in the "King March" or the "March on Washington" to rid racism and segregation from American life.[47] In like form, during the 1967 riots in the City of Newark, New Jersey "the Newark Club was very much involved in quieting areas of the city by patrolling, and talking with citizens."[48] A club member who was overtly involved in this challenging effort was Yokefellow Harry Van Dyke. His concern for stabilizing the Black community during a time when "all hell broke loose" as a result of Martin Luther King's assassination, was exemplary and in keeping with the purpose and program of the Frontiers International.

"In 1967, during the time of the riots, Jim Snead became president of the Newark Club. Under his Administration efforts were made to reduce racial tensions and to get Newark moving again. William "Bill" Ashby, who had organized and become the first director of the Urban League in the City of Newark some years earlier, helped by making contact with various organizations he had been involved with over the years."

The rebuilding of the Black community in Newark, New Jersey after the riots in the late 1960's was not only the responsibility of the men in the Frontiers Club. Their far vision and sense of equal participation helped them to establish, in 1971, the Women's Auxiliary. The latter helped in a direct way to enhance the principles of community service, and did a great deal in public service to help in the effort of stabilizing the Newark community.

One of the strongest figures in the Newark Club became the mayor of Newark, New Jersey--the Honorable Kenneth A. Gibson. His leadership, in recovering Newark from the shackles of ruin, put him into the pages of national history. He became one of America's great leaders.

Since its inception, the Newark Club produced two international presidents (i.e. James F. King and Clyde D. Mitchell); three district directors; and one international Sergeant-at-Arms.

Since 1952, the Newark Club has contributed thousands of dollars to the community. Over the past four years the club has made contributions to the Newark Fresh Air Fund, Boys and Girls clubs, Salvation Army, Newton Street School, American Legion Baseball, NAACP Golden Heritage, Black Issues Convention, Senior Citizens, Youth Christmas Parties, Scholarship awards, New Jersey State Human and Civil Rights Association; and many other community and civic organizations.

In 1988 the club developed the organizational structure for a Junior Frontiers club. Club members have been recruited and will be presented to the public at the 1989 Annual Awards Breakfast of the Newark Club. Frontiers International, Inc. President, William Joiner, wrote a letter to the Newark Club commending it for putting forth the effort to form the club.[49]

The Newark Club exemplified the highest principles of public service and has been a credit to the Frontiers organization.

The Frontiers International triumphantly walked through the pages of history as an organization of servants to community life and development. It consistently gathered into its ranks some of the most productive and dedicated personalities who believe in service to humanity and the uplifting of the down-trodden. Whether assisting the student in the classroom or the poor and homeless on the street, Frontiersmen have learned that none of their acts of generosity or kindness is ever lost but circles the earth continually in the yokeship of man's greater humanity to man.

36

The Trenton, New Jersey Frontiers Club started, as usual, with an encouraged and enthusiastic person hearing a story of goodwill from others involved in community service. William H. Dinkins, in 1953, while visiting Dayton, Ohio, came into contact with an activity sponsored by the Dayton Club. He was so impressed with the idea of community service that he influenced a group of men to form a chapter in Trenton. On July 9, 1954 22 names to be chartered were submitted to the National President, Melvin E. Farris and the Executive Secretary, Nimrod B. Allen. The chartered men were:

S.Roy Alphin
Charles C. Buford, M.D.
Roland H. Daniels, Ph.D.
William J. Dinkins, Jr.
William J. Davenport
Edward Firman
J.Herbert Gilliam
Leslie A. Hayling, D.D.S.
James W. Henderson
Joseph J. Judkins
Rubin Jones
Clifford R. Moore, Esq.
Squire J. Newsome
George H. Palmer, Jr.
Melvin Rose
Thomas Sanders
James H. Smith
J.Minor Sullivan III, M.D.
Arthur Thomas, D.D.S
Charles W. Williams, Ed.D.
Charles W. Williams
Lloyd L. Williams

There were a few others who later joined in 1954: Samuel Watts, D.D.S; Leonard J. Williams, Esq.; Frank Gonzales; Calvin Taylor; Collin Lewis, M.D.; Paul T. Williams, M.D.; John R. Marshall, M.D.; Leon Frazier, M.D.; Oscar J. Barker, Ed.D.; Charles Freeman; and James Floyd.

Some of the activities related to community service by the Trenton Club included support for the Vitiligo Foundation, the United Negro College Fund; the NAACP; the Mercer County Community College Link Project; and recognition of outstanding high school graduates from local high schools. "In addition, the Club maintained a $300 revolving fund at Trenton High School;

and supported a number of local projects and organizations (e.g., Mercer County Big Brothers and Big Sisters Organization; West End Little League; an Annual Labor Day Family Outing; and a Recognition Breakfast for the late Dr. Martin Luther King in January)."

The Trenton Club kept up the tradition of community service with high standards and hard work.[50]

History will record the great contributions of the men who call themselves Yokefellows. They have, over the years, dedicated time, voluntarily, to inner-city causes which have incessantly nagged at the minority community. Other clubs, not mentioned above, who weathered the motto, "Advancement Through Service" were: Brick's Tri-County Club made a special effort in 1973 to sponsor a fund-raising drive for the Vitiligo Fund; Christmas parties for the elderly; and support of local youth activities.[51]

Canton, Ohio Club in 1973 sponsored a city-wide party or the senior citizens of Canton; helped in a Sickle Cell Anemia program; raised money to send boys to camp; and sent donations in support of the Vitiligo Disease Research.[52]

The New Orleans Club, which was chartered in 1953, put effort into raising funds for the Vitiligo Foundation; and established a scholarship fund for needy students.[53]

The Springfield, Illinois Club supported the Vitiligo Fund; a local Boy Scouts troop; a Little League basketball team; a local school board candidate; a contribution to the Annual Boys' Club Christmas party; and sponsored a trip for Black high school students to a respected Black college in the Southern region of the country.[54]

The Nashville, Tennessee Club focused its attention around 1973-74 support of the senior citizens. The "Senior Citizens' Project" became a major effort. Transportation was supplied as a way of helping with mobility problems; and sharing time, socially, to help with difficulties associated with "loneliness," became a Yokefellow project.[55]

The Decatur club focused its volunteer concerns toward positive youth development. In this regard the club supported programs like "Self-Start," "Head-Start," and "The Frontiers Community House." Their concerns focused around decreasing juvenile delinquency; promoting an image for higher standards of living; and motivating youth from broken homes with a positive male image.[56]

38

The Saginaw Club, which began in 1954, instituted its social concerns by starting a Hall of Fame for outstanding Club Yokefellows, and instituting a tennis program and helping local youth.[57]

The Gary, Indiana Club concentrated its social concerns when it supported a civic center's programs (e.g. economic development of the minority community through fund raising activities; development of a small boat harbor for public use; and expansion of the Gary Airport.[58]

The Harrisburg, Pennsylvania Club supported a summer camp youth outreach program; sponsored a local midget league baseball team; and furnished general guidance for young people by tutoring and counseling them.[59]

Programs tackled by the Frontier's clubs have stood out, over the years, as signs of social achievement. The above examples of club service were clear indicators that volunteer service was still alive and that many residents of urban community life benefited from the noble gestures of Black men called "Yokefellows". They also represented strong positive images of academic and social achievement. Many earned college degrees or were certified skilled workers who believed that service to their fellows-in-need was a priority. There was a connective force that ignited across the country with each chapter which upheld the principle of volunteer service among those Black men who dedicated their lives to the principle of self help - a principle that remained a practice since the early 1930's.

NOTES

[1]Manuscript entitled, "The Frontiers," written by Nimrod Allen.

[2]Ibid.

[3]Ibid.

[4]Ibid.

[5]Ibid.

[6]Ibid.

[7]Ibid.

[8]Ibid.

[9]Ibid.

[10]Ibid.

[11]Ibid.

[12]Joseph S. Himes, Jr., "The Frontiers Movement," Opportunity: Journal of Negro Life, (August 1942), p. 232.

[13]Ibid.

[14]Ibid.

[15]Ibid.

[16]Ibid.

[17]Ibid.

[18]Ibid.

[19]Ibid

[20]Ibid

[21]Ibid

[22]William A. Boone, "Frontiers International: Negro Group Stresses Charity Service For All," Ebony, (Chicago: Johnson Publishing Co., 1962), p. 73.

[23]Frontiers Manual for Local Clubs, Part X, Sect. 4, p. 24, 1977.

[24]Articles from The Tennessean. Dates included: May 20, 1968; August 7, 1968; July 25, 1977; February 10, 1971; March 1968; and July 30, 1967.

[25]Article (undated) submitted by the Milwaukee club secretary.

[26]Article (undated) submitted by the Tallahassee club secretary.

[27]Article submitted by Walter S. Mills and Henry Holland, January 11, 1984.

[28]Pamphlet on the August 1963 Frontiers International Convention, held at the Sheraton-Blackstone Hotel, Chicago, Ill.

[29]Ibid.

[30]Ibid.

[31]Ibid.

[32]Ibid.

[33]Ibid.

[34]Ibid.

[35]Ibid.

[36]Ibid.

[37]A 1971 pamphlet report on the Frontiers: 31st Annual Convention, held in Springfield, Ohio.

[38]Convention pamphlet, meeting held July 20-24, 1975, at the Holiday Inn.

[39]A 35th Convention pamphlet indicating July 25-30, 1976, at the Hyatt Regency Hotel, Washington, DC.

[40]37th Convention, July 1978, Springfield, Ill., at the Forum Thirty Hotel.

[41]The Philadelphia Club Annual Report, 1978-1979, Philadelphia, Pa.

[42]45th Annual Convention pamphlet, held in Williamsburg, Va. July 16-20, 1986.

43Ibid.

[44]Historical statement from Newark Frontiers club President, Edward L. Haynes, dated February 15, 1989.

[45]Ibid.

[46]Ibid.

[47]Ibid.

[48]Ibid.

[49]Ibid.

[50]An historical statement written by W.E. Morgan, July 1, 1986, from the Trenton Club, Frontiers International.

[51]Annual District and Club Reports, 1973, a pamphlet report,p.19.

[52]Ibid., p.21.

[53]Ibid. , p.24.

[54]Ibid., p.29.

[55]An unpublished, undated statement, written by the Nashville Club secretary.

[56]Decatur Club secretary, undated statement.

[57]A written statement by the local club president, Joe T.Davis, 1974.

[58]Gary Club secretary statement, undated.

[59]Harrisburg Club secretary statement, undated.

CHAPTER IV

THE CONSTITUTION AND BY-LAWS

There was scarcely a phrase or clause of the Constitution and By-Laws of the Frontiers International which was not subjected to intense scrutiny and discussion during the organization's fifty-odd years of existence. Like fossilized bones that tell the story of long vanished civilizations, the proposed constitutional amendments, whether accepted or rejected by convention delegates, depict the problems and challenges facing the organization at particular moments in its history. Still, the document remains the organization's sole authority for being strong enough to prevent organizational disintegration, yet flexible enough to accept change.

"This Constitution," states Article XVI, Section 1, "may be amended by a two-thirds (2/3) majority of the electors present and voting at an International Convention, providing that any proposed amendments shall have first been delivered to the Executive Secretary of Frontiers International in writing at least sixty days prior to the opening of such Convention, and provided that a copy of any proposed amendments shall have been forwarded to the Secretary of each chartered club at least thirty days prior to the opening of such Convention."

A dramatic illustration of the strength of Article XVI was shown through the following three letters written November 1, 23 and December 4, respectively, of 1979.

November 1, 1979

To All Club Presidents and Secretaries
From International President

Dear Yokefellows:

As you know, our last Convention voted to increase the per capita dues for present members from $35.00 to $50.00 and for new members $40.00 to $50.00 effective January 1,1980.

Since then a significant number of clubs have expressed to me their strong opposition to these increases. They are very doubtful about being able to retain their present membership and to secure new members.

Recognizing the seriousness of the situation, I held a telephone conference meeting with the Executive Committee on October 31. The Committee voted unanimously to declare a moratorium on these changes and to retain the present dues structure until we meet in Prince Georges County in 1980.

I realize that this action is not in keeping with the Constitution as amended but be assured that we acted out of necessity for the best interest of the Organization.

For those who are not in favor of this, prepare proposed amendments to be submitted to the 1980 Convention Body.

Thank you for your understanding.

The Yokefellow,

s/Wilbert F. Singleton
t/Wilbert F. Singleton
International President

WFS/thw

46

November 23,

November 23, 1979

Wilbert Singleton, President
Frontiers International
700 North 17th Street
Harrisburg, Pennsylvania 17103

Dear President Singleton:

I was greatly distressed to receive your letter indicating that the Executive Committee had declared a moratorium on compliance with the provisions of the Constitution, raising the dues which were passed at the last general Convention and which were to go into effect on January 1, 1980. The powers of the Executive Committee are granted by Article XI, Section I of the Constitution and reads as follows:

> The President, with the consent and
> approval of the Board of Directors, shall
> appoint an Executive Committee to conduct
> business between regular meetings of the
> Board. The Executive Committee shall at
> all times be governed by the policies of
> the Board of Directors and shall name no
> powers not specifically given by the
> Board. The Executive Committee shall
> consist of five members of the Board of
> Directors, including the President and
> the International Secretary, and imme-
> diate Past President and Treasurer."

The only manner in which the Constitution may be amended is provided in Article XVI, Section I, which reads as follows:

> "This constitution may be amended by a
> two-thirds (2/3) majority of the electors
> present and voting at an International
> Convention, providing that any proposed
> amendments shall have first been deliv-
> ered to the Executive Secretary of
> Frontiers International in writing at
> least sixty days prior to the opening of
> such Convention and provided that a copy
> of any proposed amendments shall have

47

Continued from page 1

> been forwarded to the Secretary of each
> chartered club at least thirty days prior
> to the opening of such Convention."

I would strongly urge that you immediately send correspondence to the International Officers and President and Secretary of each local club, rescinding your directory of November 1, 1979 advising that an Executive Committee does not have legal authority to declare a Moratorium on provisions of the Constitution. The only body that can change the constitution is the General Convention. If any officer or group other than the General Convention assumes authority or powers not permitted by the Constitution, I have grave doubts if we will be able to continue as an organization.

Enclosed please find 20 copies of the Frontiersman.

Yours very truly,

Elmer C. Jackson, Jr.
International Attorney

ECJ,JR/kr

Cc: Robert Hill, Guy A. Jones
       Col. Gorham L. Black, Jr.
       Herbert A. Wise
       Rev. Thomas S. Logan, Sr.
       George Alford
       Rudolph Hampton
       Melwood Davis
       Julius McCoy
       James W. Davis
       Roswell O. Sutton
       A. J. Dickerson
       J. Carlton Conley
       Mel Ward

December 4, 1979

TO: All Board Members, Frontiers
     International

FROM: Wilbert F. Singleton, President

SUBJECT: Moratorium on Increase in Dues

I am sure that all of you have received a copy of the letter addressed to me by Yokefellow Elmer Jackson concerning the moratorium that was declared by the Executive Committee on the increase in dues to become effective on January 1, 1980.

As was noted in my letter to you of November 1, 1979 we realize that this action was not in keeping with the constitution.

I suppose I must take full responsibility for this action. At the time it was taken it was believed that it was in the best interest of the organization because of the many threats I had received indicating that the organization might fall apart if the dues increase was enforced. Some clubs had threatened to pull out of Frontiers. Some had stated that they would not pay the increase. Still others stated that they could not or would not attempt to get new members or look for new clubs.

When I became President, I vowed that this administration would do more to service the clubs. I believe that we have begun to do this. We are constantly in touch with the membership. We had hoped to have a Frontiersman out in September, however, it is just now coming out. We will publish another one this month. We have arranged to publish it at a considerable savings to the organization. We are ready to put a new accounting system into effect by the first of the year, as mandated by the Convention.

(2) Memo to Board Members

Plans for the 1980 Convention are well underway. And thanks to you four (4) new clubs have been formed. But be that as it may, these are not the issues at hand.

I can earnestly say that I would never abuse the Constitution. Yet, in a way, it might be said that I have not lived up to my oath to uphold the Constitution.

The Executive Committee looked at this as being one of urgency. We looked upon a moratorium as something done in a distress situation to save Frontiers.

Since this action was taken there have been communications from some praising it. On the other hand there have been those who have condemned it. I will not try to weigh one against the other, that is not important. We certainly do not want to divide the organization.

I remind you that the Amendment to the Constitution provided for the extra money to be placed in escrow for the purpose of hiring a full-time Executive Secretary whenever the Board saw fit. Even if the money was paid into escrow it could be returned to the clubs, if the Convention willed that it be done.

I must apologize for an action being taken that is contrary to the Constitution. Please do not believe that you have entrusted the leadership of Frontiers to one who will not enforce the Constitution. That is not my background. I have spent many years of living under strict rules and regulations. Please believe that I am a very dedicated person whose real concern is the success of Frontiers. I live it all day. I spend many sleepless hours at night thinking of ways to improve the organization. I will continue to do so.

Yokefellow Jackson is correct in the things he points to in his letter. I am not asking you to sanction what has been done. Rather, I want you to make the decision. If we rescind the action of the Executive Committee, which we probably should, I want you to help to convey a rationale for our action to the membership.

Since all actions are subject to the approval of the Board I plan to call a Board meeting, by telephone, at 12:00 noon on Saturday December 15, 1979.

(3) Memo to Board Members

This will include all District Directors and Counsel, Elmer Jackson. This will be the only item on the agenda unless I am notified by any of you, in writing, prior to the conference call of something of an urgent nature that needs to be discussed.

Please notify Mrs. Thelma Harris Williams if you will be at a number other than the one she has listed for you.

s/W.FS
President

Note: If you have not voted for the Secretary, please send in your card at once. My latest count indicated that only 8 out of 15 had voted.
s/S.

Some illustrations of the Constitution's flexibility to changes in American cultural and social patterns are shown below:

CONCERNING WOMEN'S RIGHTS

In 1962, Article V, Section 2, read:
"Active membership in this club shall be limited to <u>male</u> <u>persons</u> twenty-one years of age or over. . ."

In 1988, it was amended to read: "Active membership in this club shall be limited to <u>persons</u> twenty-one years of age or over. . ."

During that 26-year span many attempts were made to pass an amendment which would grant women full Frontiers membership status. The following editorial in the Frontiersman newsletter of April 1975 by Yokefellow Elmer C. Jackson, Jr., the International Attorney, describes the organization's dilemma:

As I have read and observed the work of various service organizations throughout the country, including Frontiers International, I cannot help but recognize the great loss of potential for service in failing to utilize the talents of women as full-fledged members.

I'm aware that the By-Laws of Frontiers provide for the organization of Women's Auxiliaries to clubs throughout the country, but feel that club membership and achievements may be doubled or even tripled if membership rolls were opened to women.

In this age of Women's Liberation it may be well to observe that the organized church is one of the most active and productive service institutions in modern society, and no one needs to tell us who the major workers are. Think about it.

Despite the enlightened view expressed above, until the July 1988 Convention all attempts to amend the Constitution to include women members failed, largely because members present and voting held the unshakable belief that the Yokefellows "back home" would never accept women except as auxiliary members.

Also, for years a battle raged between the clubs and the International office. The International's expenses included public relations and travel expenses, clerking salaries, media and yearly Convention expenses, publishing the Frontiers quarterly newsletter, and all incidental expenses attached to renting and maintaining a facility adequate to serve as an International headquarters. All of the funds needed by the International had to be generated through its clubs, and the clubs, in turn, felt that the only way to maintain a strong, paid-up membership was to keep the membership fee as low as possible.

In 1961 a compromise was reached and Article XII, Section 5 of the Local Club By-Laws was amended to the following:

> Each chartered club is required to contribute
> annually to the International Office ten
> percent (10%) of the net income from each
> fund raising,project or $100.00, whichever is
> the greater.

In 1962, Harold L. Pilgrim, the International Executive Secretary, wrote the following to the International Board of Directors regarding the ten percent project:

> This supporting arm of our activities is openly
> being violated by our constituency. Some promote
> projects and do not report to our office, others,
> after the promotion of projects, on a purely
> arbitrary basis, forward what their minds dictate,
> if and when they desire.
>
> Agencies outside the Frontiers receive from our
> clubs in most instances greater financial support
> than the International Organization itself; serious
> consideration should be given to a reversal of this
> kind of thought and action; if not, this movement
> will wind up with the "tail wagging the dog"
> instead of being the other way around.

A 1963 report revealed that the new law was unpopular and ineffective. Of the 58 clubs which existed at that time 24 had rendered some support and 34 had made no contribution. Active clubs, who sponsored frequent fund-raising events, were bearing an unfair burden simply because they were active.

By 1973 the Frontiers International Constitution and its By-laws had been amended, and the unpopular (10%) revenue assessment had been removed. However, to compensate for that loss in revenue for the International, the membership dues were increased. The precedent for the ratification of constitutional laws by people other than those persons in authority was not an idea created by a few members of the Frontiers International. As far as the American constitutional process was concerned, James Madison gave the initial call for "ratification by the people" of those combined laws which were called the U.S. Constitution (1787). His position, which, as history revealed, did not become a part of the ratification process, but did suggest that the states would have power over the central government if the people did not receive the ultimate power to accept laws.

If the states ratified the new constitution, then in the future, if there was ever a conflict between the states and the central government, it would seem that the states had the ultimate authority, that they could repudiate what they had originally agreed to - that if the states created the federal government, they would have the power to dismantle it or withdraw from it. The new government must be ratified by 'the supreme authority' of the people themselves. Then the states (or the central government, for that matter) could not set aside what the people had made.[1]

Around 1818, when laws were not as aggravated by a populated bureaucracy as they are today in America, the position that James Madison took on a government "by the people" had more impact. In regards to a state having power that might refute the authority of the federal government, the position of the people petitioning through their representatives set a precedent under the Constitution. The Chief Justice of the Supreme Court at that time, John Marshall, suggested:

The government proceeds directly from the people; is "ordained and established" in the name of the people.... The assent of the States in their sovereign capacity, is implied in calling a Convention, and thus submitting that instrument to the people. But the people were at perfect liberty to accept or reject it; and their act was final. It required not the affirmance, and could not be negatived, by the State governments. The constitution, when thus adopted was of complete obligation, and bound the State sovereignties.[2]

Chief Justice Marshall merely fortified the argument made by James Madison and James Wilson during the Constitutional Convention: "the federal government must be a government that derives its power and purpose from the people as a whole and the only way to transcend state rivalries was to make the United States a nation of people, not of states."[3]

It appears that the Frontiers International has benefitted from the earlier U.S. Constitutional practices, i.e. it is at a convention, where people are voting, that laws are amended, and representatives holding offices of authority can carry them out. No single club chapter, like no single state (e.g. as precedented in 1818) could make a ruling unless the people voted (i.e. in an organized convention) and their representatives have carried out their wishes through constitutional law.

In a country like the United States where there is a "thin line" that enters the picture when rules and laws are established by the federal government and the "will of the people", one must look back at those events, which "in the course of human events" in American politics which have created two great documents that we live by today. The Declaration of Independence (1776), and the U.S. Constitution (1787), struggled through trial and error, to set limits on the will and conscience where "the people" and "the government authority" were concerned. The words were clear in the Declaration:

That to secure these rights, Governments are instituted among men, deriving their just powers from the consent of the governed.

That whenever any form of Government becomes destructive of these ends, it is the Right of the People to alter or to abolish it, and to institute new government....

In order to make the Declaration more formidable and make the relationship between "the people" and "the government" more workable, the U.S. Constitution brought a clearer understanding of who, why, and by what procedure laws were to be established.

The primary focus of the U.S. Constitution, as it substantiated the rights and privileges of citizens to give input into it through representatives, was through the amending process. Citizens, through their congressional representatives, were able to see that new laws of governance were added to the main document.

One writer put the relationship between the Constitution and the Amendments clearly. He suggested that "most of the twenty-four current amendments to the Constitution of the United States actually have little to do with the Constitution itself. . . Sixteen, including the Bill of Rights, are devoted to providing or extending the rights of citizens-subjects totally absent from the basic Constitution."[4]

Furthermore, "the fact that the amendments have altered the Constitution so little does not mean that they are or ever were minor or unimportant. The promise of the first ten helped prevent the defeat of the Constitution. They and the others have been vitally important in the growth and history of the United States."[5]

Through the precedent of a solid historical past, and an image of persistent involvement "of the people", the membership of the Frontiers International continue to follow the pattern set by the ardent pioneers of American constitutional law. Members continue to play major roles, state by state, and town by town, in the constitutional strength of the organization.

NOTES

[1]Charles L. Mee, Jr., <u>The Genius of the People</u>, (N.Y. Harper & Row, Publishers, 1987), pp.134-135.

[2]Fred W. Friendly and Martha J.H. Elliot, <u>The Constitution: That Delicate Balance</u> , (N.Y.: Random House, 1984), p.259.

[3]Ibid, p.260.

[4]Charles Leedham, <u>Our Changing Constitution</u>, (N.Y.: Dodd, Mead & Co., 1964), p.1.

[5]Ibid., p.2.

CHAPTER V

FRONTIERS AND VITILIGO

Mrs. Pearlena E. Jackson of Newark, New Jersey, had just had an operation. She was 42, physically attractive, about five feet five, with a smooth chocolate-brown complexion, and a smile that betrayed that her lot was cast on the bright side of life. She didn't drink, and she was enthusiastic about church, but she was no "goody twoshoes." She liked dancing and bowling, and she did both well.

After the operation began to heal, a white patch about the size of a quarter appeared on Pearlena's abdomen. Her doctor said it would disappear, and she believed him. It didn't disappear, but it didn't grow, nor did it hurt; it was out of sight, and she eventually forgot about it. Then, 10 years later, she awakened one morning to find a large white spot around her mouth--and she burst into tears. Why would God let this happen to her? For some time she would not go out, but the continual spread of the disease forced her out to seek medical help.

Pearlena was surprised to find how few physicians knew anything about the disease. It was spreading on her rapidly now. The spot around her mouth had widened to cover her chin. Her eyebrows and underlids, hair and scalp, hands and wrists, legs and ankles, were blotched white. Even her buttocks had been ravaged by the disease, making her into the caricature of a "vitiligo-ized Playboy Bunny." Nearly half of her body now was milk-white, the remainder, chocolate-brown.[1]

To say that people were concerned about her appearance would be to grossly understate the situation. She had lost her job and spent all of her money taking medication that succeeded only in making her sick. People backed away from her on elevators and buses. At a store a woman clerk took a bill from her hand, then looked up into her face in horror and literally threw money back in gross overpayment before rushing away. Pearlena wanted to correct the error, but realizing the woman's panic was caused by her appearance, left the store quietly with the extra money. She tried to laugh it off, but it hurt, and it hurt worse when a dermatologist finally told her flatly, "Eventually you will turn all white!"[2]

Forced to seek employment, she was turned down on job after job until one personnel officer took her aside, and said, "Give it up, Mrs. Jackson. No company will hire you. Their other employees would be afraid of you, and no company insurance would ever cover you. You'd better try to get Social Security Disability Insurance Benefits."[3]

In spite of assurances by doctors that vitiligo (which they had finally discovered her illness to be) was not contagious, even members of her immediate family now operated at a distance. On one occasion, when her only daughter was sporting a new boyfriend, Pearlena's sister projected herself as "mother." "What hurt most," Pearlena says, "was that my daughter said nothing to correct it!"

At her Social Security hearing on her disability application the Administrative Law Judge said, "She looks like a freak!" Though the case was decided in her favor, his words burned like a whip across the sensitive skin of her courage.

She owned her own bowling ball, and she still went to the alleys until one day a man approached her and offered her $20 for a date. When she refused civilly, he said, "Lady, the way you look you should be glad to go out with anybody!"

It was her church that came to her rescue. Rev. James Perry and the congregation of the Missionary Baptist Church had missed her and came to find her.

"They were not afraid of me." she said. "They threw their arms around me and I needed that human touch. Pastor Perry said, 'Keep coming to church and the Lord will give you strength.'"[4]

"I began to pray again, and almost as an answer I heard about the Frontiers International and all they were doing about vitiligo. I found out about Dr. William Anderson of East Orange, and I talked with Dr. John Kenney, Dr. Harold Minus, and Dr. Pearl Grimes, the dermatologists at Howard University. They're a wonderful group. I know someday through Frontiers research somebody will find a cure for vitiligo. I'm a spokesman for them now. I go out to talk to many groups with Fred Stalks who heads the Frontier vitiligo program here in Newark. I'm taking therapy myself and I know I've improved, and I'm going to help them all I can!"

60

"Vitiligo," says Dr. John A. Kenney, Jr., the retired Professor and Chairman, Department of Dermatology, Howard University and Freedmen's Hospital, Washington, D. C., "has always been with man. There is evidence that the skin disorder afflicted man during biblical times. Early Egyptians had it. In India, if a spouse should get it, it's grounds for divorce. No one in India will marry a person afflicted with this disease."[5]

In the United States, among a certain segment of the Black population, the belief is still prevalent that "when the last spot on the body turns white, the person dies."[6]

Two percent of the world's population, roughly fifty to a hundred million people, suffered from it, and vitiligo shows no sex, age, race, or class predilection. Some vitiligo (pronounced vit-a-lie-go) patients even suffered a loss of pigment in the retina of the eye.[7]

For some unknown reason the skin of the vitiligo victim lost the ability to pigment normally, leading to milk-white splotches as if the skin had been burnt. It was progressive, like the graying of hair. It generally showed up first on the exposed areas of the body, face and back of hands and around body openings. In addition to persons it also affected horses, cows, pigs, and elephants.[8]

The cause of vitiligo was not known. One theory was that abnormally functioning nerve cells injure adjacent pigment cells. This theory applied to cases of generalized and segmental vitiligo (pigment loss in a region supplied by facial or other nerves). Another theory was based on the fact that under some circumstances the body would destroy its own tissue (an autoimmune reaction). In this case the pigment within the cells was destroyed in response to a substance the body perceives as foreign. What triggered this response and why "defensive" cells release toxins that destroy cell pigment was not known. Other disorders frequently associated with vitiligo and which may have involved a similar reaction were thyroiditis, diabetes mellitus, and pernicious anemia.

Another theory under investigation was that pigment producing cells were self-destructive (autocytotoxic). In the normal synthesis of pigment cells the body produced by-products that were highly toxic and which, in turn, destroyed pigment cells. Exactly how this feedback mechanism differed in normal individuals and vitiligo patients was not understood.[9]

In some cases, such as chemical vitiligo, the initial destruction of the cells originated outside the body. Chemical vitiligo, occurring after exposure

61

to some germicidal agents, was an example of how the destructive action of a chemical on pigment cells could be reinforced by the body's defense mechanism. In this type of pigment loss, the cells that have been destroyed by the chemical released a substance that triggered production of the antibodies. These antibodies attacked the remaining healthy pigment cells and further loss of pigment occurred.[10]

Understanding this kind of immunologic involvement was especially important in treating patients with melanomas (cancer of the pigment-producing cells), who had ten to twenty times the normal incidence of vitiligo. Some melanoma patients seemed to develop specific antibodies that made them more susceptible to substances such as those that trigger vitiligo.[11]

At the request of Nimrod B. Allen, Emmer Martin Lancaster (the late and long-time Foundation Director), presented the initial vitiligo proposal to the Ninth National Frontiers Convention in Atlantic City, New Jersey, July 27-29, 1950, at the Arctic Avenue Branch YMCA. Said Lancaster:

> In the event this national objective is approved and in operation, it would establish the Frontiers Club as the first national Negro service organization to initiate a national foundation for health service to the Negro public; the first service organization within the race to present a specific grant to a Negro university for health study and research; and the first Negro service group to initiate a national project for curative study in an unexplored field of medical science.
>
> It is admitted that there are other national objectives with greater popular appeal than the vitiligo project. Service to youth in the form of scholarships and attention to juvenile delinquency problems have a far greater dramatic appeal to the public than the proposed project. However, these fields of endeavor are already explored and supported by private and public philanthropy, and our connection therewith would be as supporting contributors. The name Frontiers signifies "new and unexplored realms of

62

thought and research;" it connotes the
pioneer aspects of adventure and discovery.
Accordingly, the vitiligo project stamps the
Frontiers Club as a primal factor in a new
field, rather than a contributory agent to
already existing areas of national effort.[12]

The adoption of the vitiligo medical project was delayed until the 12th
Frontiers Convention in Dayton, Ohio, 1953, at which time Frontiers delegates
approved the vitiligo medical research proposal as their official national
project and simultaneously authorized the Board of Directors, as
recommended in the original proposal, to establish a National Research
Charitable Corporation to administer the vitiligo research project.

Pursuant to the authorization of the Dayton Frontiers Convention, the
Board of Directors and the Executive Committee of Frontiers of America
convened jointly in Washington, D.C., January 30, 1954, and formed the
National Frontiers Vitiligo Foundation, Incorporated. Freedmen's Hospital
(Howard University) of Washington, D.C., was selected as the medical facility
"to conduct research and therapy to determine the symptoms, causes,
treatment, prevention, and cure of vitiligo." A medical research fund of
$10,000 was initially authorized by the 13th Frontiers Convention in
Washington, D.C., July 29-31, 1954, to finance the vitiligo research project.

The certificate of incorporation was approved and recorded in the
District of Columbia on the 22nd day of March 1954. As expressed in the
certificate, the purpose and objectives of the foundation are:

1. To stimulate, coordinate, and
sponsor scientific research to determine the
symptoms, causes, treatment, prevention, and
cure of vitiligo.

2. To provide financial assistance in
the form of voluntary contributions to
universities, hospitals, medical schools, and
other medical research institutions for the
purpose of diagnostic treatment and allevia-
tion, prevention, and cure of vitiligo.[13]

Frontiers International Vitiligo Foundation is regarded as "the only
organized group of individuals In the nation who has formally established a
foundation for this purpose and who has and is taking a special interest in this
disease."[14] This Foundation had contributed annually to the Medical College

of Howard University for research and therapy, to determine the cause and cure of vitiligo.

The $10,000 grant to Howard University's College of Medicine in 1954 marked the beginning of a long relationship. Under Dr. John A. Kenney, Jr., much progress was made in the field of research. Dr. Kenney discovered that vitiligo can be treated by a trial and error method. A drug called psoralen is either taken orally or painted (alcohol tincture) on the depigmented areas. In both cases the skin was exposed to ultraviolet light (sunlight) from two to fifteen minutes. The one to three year treatment was effective with some patients but not with others. At Howard University the cost was $12 per visit (private dermatologists charge $40 per visit).

From 1960, Frontiers had contributed at least $2,000 additionally each year. In later years the yearly contribution was raised to $5,000.

Through the heroically persistent sponsorship of Congressman Parren J. Mitchell of Baltimore, Maryland, in April 1979 the federal government agency, National Institutes of Health (NIH) awarded a four-year research grant of $2 million for vitiligo research. The grant culminated four years of intense effort: persuading committee chairmen to get the "Mitchell Bill" (otherwise known as the National Vitiligo Control Act H.R. 5264-65) out of the committee for public hearing--vitiligo kits for all congressmen--conferences between Dr. Kenney and dermatologists of the NIH--starting a companion bill in the senate--persuading the Chairman of the National Democratic Party to include the bill in the national platform, etc.

This grant was awarded to a consortium of institutions consisting of Yale University, Howard University, Bryn Mawr College and the University of Pennsylvania, the University of Massachusetts, and the Massachusetts Eye and Ear Infirmary of Boston, Massachusetts.[15]

Areas of research were designated as follows: Dr. Aaron B. Lerner and Dr. James J. Nordlund, Yale University School of Medicine and Vitiligo Projects Coordinators, established a clinical center for vitiligo patients to study principally the relationship of vitiligo to other diseases such as autoimmunity and melanomas and their treatment.

Dr. John A. Kenney, Howard University, had, through the assistance of Frontiers International, already established a clinical center with a general objective of determining symptoms, causes, treatment, prevention, and the ultimate cure of vitiligo.[16]

The University of Pennsylvania and Bryn Mawr College specialized on the sociological and psychological effects of vitiligo, and the Massachusetts institutions conducted studies to determine the relationship of vitiligo to defects of vision and other abnormal conditions of vitiligo patients' eyes.

Congressman Mitchell also introduced a bill permanently earmarking funds for vitiligo research, and since the initial grant the NIH has renewed the original commitment successively for three-year periods on a conditional basis. The consortium's grant as of 1987 is approximately $350,000 per year.

In the 37 years which have passed since Emmer Lancaster recommended that Frontiers extend a helping hand to the sufferers of vitiligo many changes have occurred. At Howard University Dr. John Kenney (the vitiligo pioneer) retired and was succeeded as Department of Dermatology Chairman by Dr. Harold R. Minus. Dr. Pearl Grimes moved to Martin Luther King, Jr. Hospital in Los Angeles, and at Howard's Freedmen's Hospital Dr. Rebat Halder became Director of the Vitiligo Research Center. In January 1984 Emmer Lancaster passed away and he was succeeded as Director of the Frontiers Vitiligo Foundation by Yokefellow Robert L. Johnson. On Capitol Hill the retirement of Congressman Mitchell removed a strong supporting arm for vitiligo funding at a time when federal funds for social and health needs have been drastically reduced and of those available, life threatening diseases like AIDS are commanding the major share.

Yet, every coin has two sides. The doctors, politicians, and Yokefellows who have passed on or retired have been replaced by men equally as competent, equally as dedicated. In 1950 few dermatologists had even heard of vitiligo. Now, through the efforts of Frontiers one can get treatment for it in Alabama, California, Connecticut, Georgia, Illinois, Indiana, Maryland, New York, New Jersey, Nebraska, Ohio, Pennsylvania, Tennessee, Texas, and the District of Columbia. According to Dr. Halder: Howard University doctors see about 120 vitiligo patients each week. They came from the District of Columbia, Virginia, Maryland, and Pennsylvania. "We also run an international referral center with patients coming from such places as Brazil, Ethiopia, and Kuwait."

In 1950, the Vitiligo Foundation was considered as merely one brick in the vast building structure of the Frontiers International, but by the 1980s the sheer numbers of afflicted who had come forward, and the desperation expressed in their appeals for help had forcibly moved vitiligo from periphery status to the position of a cornerstone of the Frontiers organization.

In 1980 Frontiers established its Vitiligo Courtesy Club, honoring with a bronze plaque those contributing $500 or more and honoring with a certificate of appreciation those contributing at least $100 to the cure of this disease. Presentations are made at the annual convention.

"If it meant getting it off me," a man from Duquesne, Pennsylvania, wrote to Dr. Kenney, "I would travel a million miles. . . . It's really painful down deep when I think about it--and that's every day. . . "[17]

Appeals like the one above, and courageous spirits like Mrs. Pearlena Jackson, have hardened the resolve of the Frontiersmen and the doctors of Howard and other universities and medical institutions, that somehow, sometime, somewhere a cure for vitiligo must be found!

In the middle 1980s the legal counsel of the Frontiers International brought to the attention of the governing body the fact that the Frontiers International, Inc., and the National Frontiers Vitiligo Foundation, Inc., had the same Board of Directors and management and as such were indistinguishable corporate entities holding different tax exemption status.

To correct the discrepancy the old Vitiligo Foundation was dissolved and in 1988 a new organization, the Frontiers International Foundation, Incorporated, "FIFI" was born. The new Foundation had a new Board of Directors and a new set of By-Laws, its relationship to Frontiers International being maintained initially by the fact that the majority of FIFI's Board of Directors are Yokefellows or Yokettes.

FIFI was an umbrella Foundation that permits Frontiers International to support the research and treatment of the multiple diseases which affect primarily the Black community, such as vitiligo, sickle-cell anemia, and hypertension. It also permitted the Foundation to solicit, collect, receive, acquire, hold, and invest money and property. However, despite the broadened perspectives, the cure for vitiligo remains the new Foundation's top research priority. Like the Frontiers Clubs themselves, the original Foundation was born out of human suffering, and in this continued search for cures for human ills lies Frontiers International's best hope for a brighter tomorrow.

NOTES

[1]Interview of Pearlena E. Jackson, in Newark, New Jersey, by Fred Johnson, January 1987.

[2]Ibid.

[3]Ibid.

[4]Ibid.

[5]Mack Alexander, "Black Club, Clinic Fight Disease That Whitens Skin," The Kansas City Star, Thursday, July 18, 1974, p.3.

[6]Ibid.

[7]Ibid.

[8]U. S. Department of Health and Human Services, "What You Should Know About Vitiligo," NIH Publication No. 80-2088, July 1980.

[9]Ibid.

[10]Ibid.

[11]Ibid.

[12]Emmer Martin Lancaster, "A National Project for The Frontiers Club of America," Washington, D.C., June 9, 1950.

[13]Certificate of Incorporation, District of Columbia, March 1954.

[14]A research paper entitled "Federal Government Sponsors First Vitiligo Workshop," undated and unsigned, and released by the National Institute of Health, March 1977, p.2.

[15]National Frontiers Vitiligo Foundation, Inc. "Annual Report," June 30, 1986.

[16]Alexander, Op, cit.

[17]Ibid.

CHAPTER VI

WOMEN'S AUXILIARY: THE YOKETTES

A poem, written by the noted black poet and writer, Langston Hughes, depicts the encouragement and backing of wives and women supporters of the Frontiersmen: patience, love, concern and dedication to the work of community service and family unity.

MOTHER TO SON

Well, son, I'll tell you:
Life for me ain't been no crystal
      stair.
It's had tacks in it,
And splinters,
And boards torn up,
And places with no carpet on
      the floor -
Bare.
But all the time
I'se been a-climbin' on,
And reachin' landin's,
And turnin' corners,
And sometimes goin' in the dark
Where there ain't been no light.
So boy, don't you turn back.
Don't you set down on the steps
'Cause you finds it's kinder hard.
Don't you fall now -
For I'se still goin', honey,
I'se still climbin' ,
And life for me ain't been no
      Crystal stair.[1]

Langston Hughes

It seemed that Black women in American history spent much of their spare time supporting and backing causes instituted by Black men. The Frontiers International, Incorporated owed much of its success to the efforts of Black women throughout the country who were active in the women's counterpart of the Frontiers International known as Yokettes. Women in America had often been stigmatized as secondary role players in the work force. The enthusiastic participation of many women in volunteer organizations had been overlooked as a factor in organizational skill development. Many Black women, who have shown remarkable leadership ability in the Frontiers Auxiliary, were capable of serving in challenging political, economic and educational roles. Margaret Hennig and Anne Jordin, in their book The Managerial Woman, suggested that "many women automatically, without thinking, discount what they have done."[2]

The unique classification of those Black women who have volunteered their services as Yokettes was indicative of their family and community association and dedication. They have not realized, as a group, that their skill in program development has helped their male counterparts keep the organization thriving throughout the years. The psychology that often came into play clearly supports the behavior of those women who have given of their time away from family and work responsibilities. Toni Cade Bambara described the image here suggested in her book The Black Woman:

> Our first perception of ourselves is of
> our physical bodies, which we are then forced
> to compare with the bodies of those with whom
> we live, mothers, fathers, grandmothers,
> aunts, uncles, and whomever. Our clothing
> and the kinds of play activity we engage in
> are reflections of the lives of those with
> whom we live.[3]

We can take from this perceptive statement the idea that the dedicated women, who have offered their time and energy to make community service a reality through the Frontiers' organization were brought up in homes, or came into contact with special people in their upbringing, where volunteer service and the spirit of giving were standard principles.

According to the organization's Constitution, the official name for the women was "Women's Auxiliaries of the Frontiersmen International, an arm of Frontiers International, Inc."[4] The women, who have played active roles, over the years, as support workers called "Yokettes," were not playing secondary roles. They have been, and still are, co-workers and equal partners in the concept of working for community service with the men. The various roles that women have played in Frontiers auxiliaries have been instrumental in the survival and strength of the organization.

The representative body of the women's auxiliary was labeled "Coordinating Council of the Women's Auxiliaries of Frontiersmen." It was organized "to act as a pool for sifting and synthesizing ideas, procedures and plans, which may be shared with local auxiliaries in the implementation of their programs at the local level."[5]

The Council had the specific responsibility, as it attempted to establish auxiliaries in communities around the country, "to provide stimulation and guidance;"[6] "to provide direction. . . suggest activities and prospects" that would enhance the Frontiers' image in the local community; "to work with designated Frontiers representatives on questions of development and emerging responsibilities."[7]

Structurally, the Council was set up on a standard basis indicative of mature and stable organizational habits, i.e., a president, vice president, recording secretary, corresponding secretary, financial secretary, treasurer, chaplain, parliamentarian and an historian. Added to this outline were two advisors who were the last two immediate past presidents.[8] Each officer was assigned specific duties to be carried out with vigor, trust and loyalty to the organization; the purpose of this being to assure not only a positive image to the community, but a sense of dedication to the needs of the local community. To assure that the image and spirit of the auxiliary were maintained, a "National Hymn" was created using the tune taken from "Auld Lang Syne:"

> Should we forget our yesterdays
> And what we said we'd do.
> We were so few and far apart
> Our work was also new,
> Advancement Through Service, yes,
> We could not fall behind,
> Continuing as the years rolled by
> With aims we kept in mind.
>
> We knew we had to reach our aims,
> Advancement our game;
> No matter what would slow
> our pace
> Our strength would be the same.
> Examples for the ones to come,
> Yes, striving day by day;
> Together we could serve the cause

"Advancement" yes, we'd say.

No fear can stop our plan or plot,
We're moving right along;
We'll work together day and night,
To get where we belong.
The future calls for standards high,
Our aims are big, not small;
Advancement for our task each time,
We will wait the call.[9]

These words of dedication and service were put together by Sara W. Dickerson. The view, as she here expressed in song, was expressive of how women, who served in Frontiers Auxiliary chapters, throughout the country, felt about uplifting their local communities and being of service to those persons who could not help themselves.

In 1978-79 there emerged a list of active, chartered auxiliaries throughout the country which was indicative of the spirit and public support that women (related in some way to their Yokefellow counterparts) gave. Their theme, during that time period, labeled by the Coordinating Council of Women's Auxiliaries, was "Community Involvement... The Black Woman's Challenge." The chartered auxiliaries at that time were:

Akron, Ohio	Decatur, Illinois
Annapolis, Maryland	Dover, Delaware
Atlantic City, New Jersey	Harrisburg, Pennsylvania
Baltimore, Maryland	Houston, Texas
Buck's Tri-County, N.C.	Kansas City, Missouri
Canton, Ohio	Lafayette, Louisiana
Lima, Ohio	Philadelphia, Pennsylvania
Mercer County, Pennsylvania	Prince George's County,
Milwaukee, Wisconsin	Maryland
Nashville, Tennessee	Saginaw, Michigan
Newark, New Jersey	Shelbyville, Tennessee
Omaha, Nebraska	Springfield, Illinois
Opelousas, Louisiana	Springfield, Ohio

Officers were (1978-79)

International President	Francine B. Freeman
Vice President	Roberta Alford
Recording Secretary	Electa Holland
Corresponding Secretary	Alma Fletcher

72

Financial Secretary	Norma Ford
Treasurer	Louise Jackson
Parliamentarian	Isabelle Jackson
Chaplain	Carlene Gundy
Immediate Past President	Sara Dickerson
Advisor	Barbara Martin[10]

Public service was not a constrained practice for some of the ladies listed above. It was their pioneering and community volunteer spirit which assisted their enthusiasm and active involvement in the Frontier movement. On March 5, 1977, for example, Sara W. Dickerson, President of the Frontiers International Auxiliaries at that time, was elected to the Advisory Board of the Salvation Army, Houston Club in Houston, Texas. In a special report the installation ceremony was elaborately described:

> The Salvation Army Advisory Board held their
> Annual Meeting and Luncheon, with Harry G.
> Austin, Chairman, presiding. Invocation was
> given by Rabbi Myron Judah Schachtel, of
> Congregation Beth Israel. The installation
> of new officers and members was conducted by
> the Salvation Army City Commander, Major
> Ralph G. Merrel. Following the luncheon, the
> address was given by Major Jack Waters.[11]

Sara Dickerson's role in her new volunteer post with the Salvation Army focused on working to assure that more people around the Houston area would be reached and made aware of the program's effort to meet the needs of the hungry, poor and destitute citizens. It was this pioneering spirit that she brought to the Frontiers and modeled for other women to follow.

PHILADELPHIA, PENNSYLVANIA

The woman of Frontiers added another feather in the hat of Willie Penn in the city of "brotherly love" in 1952 when the newly formed auxiliary met at the Eleventh Annual Convention, held July 31 to August 1, 1952. Nimrod Allen, founder, might have been the initiator of the idea to include women in the organization. He "sent a letter to the officers of the Philadelphia Chapter suggesting that some planned social activity was needed to provide entertainment for the wives who accompanied their husbands to the convention site. Philadelphia wives were invited to attend a meeting at the home of Mr. and Mrs. Adolphia Lewis."[12] As a result of this informal gathering, the ladies present planned several meetings and scheduled some

73

social events "which would be subsidized by both the men and the ladies." They planned a garden party at the home of Dr. and Mrs. W. M. Cousins; an evening reception at the Plaisted Boat House on East River Drive; and an affair held on a large estate about 25 miles from Philadelphia called "Longview."[13] The success of these events was not social, but achieved two purposes. First, they inspired the men of the Frontiers to support the idea of a women's auxiliary chapter. And second, to gather ideas for funding, charity and community service by women who would subsequently support their male counterparts in these ventures, was concrescent.

The Philadelphia Chapter of the women's auxiliary (members were later referred to as "Yokettes") was the first group of its type nationally. It wasn't until 1956 that a committee of Yokefellows (men) was selected by the National President, Donald Crawford, to promote women's auxiliaries in the local men's chapters. In 1957, at Newark, New Jersey, a plan was submitted which authorized Frontiers chapters throughout the country to organize women's auxiliaries in their respective communities "if the local men's clubs so desired."[14]

The national Office of Frontiers International was still under the direction of its founder, Nimrod Allen. Allen and his executive secretary, Harold L. Pilgrim, "had granted several charters by the year 1961 to the existing women's auxiliaries."[15] In that same year, at its national convention, the Frontiers' ruling delegates resolved, officially, to form a national organization of auxiliaries. The sponsor of the resolution was Dr. Bernard Harris of Baltimore, Maryland, who was given the responsibility of seeing that the information was properly disseminated. A Dr. Joseph A. Wiseman was appointed to coordinate those auxiliaries that established charters, which were: Philadelphia, Pennsylvania; Baltimore, Maryland; Annapolis, Maryland; Prince George's County, Maryland; and Columbus, Ohio.[16]

The first formal meeting of the newly chartered Philadelphia auxiliary was held in 1962 at the Philadelphia National Convention. Common consensus at the meeting expressed a loosely structured organization so that open communication and cooperation with other auxiliaries would be commonplace. "This informal plan would allow representation of each auxiliary to participate in developing guidelines for convention programs while simultaneously promoting cooperation and friendship among the ladies of Frontiers chapters."[17] It was in this spirit that the Coordinating Council was born, officers were chosen, and a more structured format for convention meetings was devised, i.e., a business session and seminar meetings.[18]

In 1963 at the Chicago, Illinois Convention, the first formal election was conducted and a new constitution and handbook were approved. The elected officers were:

President	: Katharine Dockens, Philadelphia, Pa.
Vice President	: Ethel Harris, Baltimore, Md.
Recording Sec.	: Mildred Nall, Annapolis, Md.
Treasurer	: Mildred Gray, Prince George's County, Md.
Historian	: Clara Allen, Columbus, Oh.
Coordinator	: Dr. Joseph Wiseman, Annapolis, Md.[19]

As of 1986 there were 23 women's auxiliary clubs of the Frontiers across America. The Philadelphia Club set a historical precedent for the women's involvement in the Frontiers movement. They remain today a viable, productive and provocative organization who donate a great deal of time and resource to community concerns.

Beginning with its chartered status in 1963 and years following a list of coordinating presidents were documented:

Katharine Dockens	Philadelphia, Pa.
Ernestine Johnson	Baltimore, Md.
Barbara F. Martin	Prince George's County, Md.
Vera Clemmons	Opelousas, La.
Sara Dickerson	Houston, Tx.
Francine Freeman	Prince Georges County, Md.
Roberta Alford	Newark, N.J.
Ruth Easley	Philadelphia Pa.
Cleo Turner	Enfield, N.C.
Mildred Hill	Omaha, Ne.
Alma J. Fletcher	Glendale, Md.[20]

BALTIMORE

As the spirit of public service across the country began to spread among the spouses of the Frontiersmen, "a flame caught fire" in the souls of wives and female friends in Baltimore, Maryland. Out of this desire to heighten the volunteer services to community, "the Women's Auxiliary of Frontiers International of Baltimore, Maryland was organized in June 1959."[21] At its organizational meeting Edna Over Gray Campbell, Vice Principal of Douglas High School in Baltimore, spoke. Her words represented the vision of those women present. Part of her speech was recorded in the local newspaper. In her speech she was quick to say, "A man's organization never gets in stride until it gets women pushing it along."[22] She further suggested in the news article that an auxiliary should take on the role as "assistant, aide or ally, never subordinate" to the male Frontiers. She envisioned a group of women who exercised interest in franchise, i.e. assure that blacks would register and vote; also "housing integration, renewal problems, and service to community groups, hospitals."[23]

The Baltimore auxiliary was the fourth chapter organized, following Dayton, Ohio; Columbia, Maryland; and Prince Georges County, Maryland. The officers elected on the evening of June 1959 were:

President	: Beatrice Pitts
Vice President	: Annie Mae Gittings
Recording Sec.	: Elizabeth Henderson
Corres. Sec.	: Irene Day
Financial Sec.	: Frances Rideout
Treasurer	: Bennie Poey[24]

"The charter for the club was subsequently received July 28, 1960."[25]

According to the club's constitution, membership consisted of wives, widows and unmarried daughters of financial Frontiersmen; and ladies who have, upon the club's recommendation, been named Honorary Members.[26]

It was under Beatrice Pitts' leadership that the auxiliary club established itself as a solid service organization. They adopted the Upton School as their Major Service Project. It presented Grace Bumbry, a noted singer, in her American premiere, in concert at the Lyric Theatre on October 16, 1962. It served, also, as official hostesses for all the events sponsored by the auxiliary and Frontiers club. A great achievement was awarded the auxiliary when they made a sizeable financial contribution in the organization's name to a local hospital in Maryland, the New Provident Hospital.[27]

From 1970-73 officers elected were:

President	: Thelma C. Moore
Vice President	: Carlene Gundy
Recording Sec.	: Ethel Davis
Treasurer	: Beatrice Pitts[28]

It was during the 1970-73 administration that a <u>Pictorial Booklet</u> was initiated into print. As a way of continuing service to community projects, financial contributions were made to two foundations; Vitiligo, and Sickle Cell

76

Anemia. A special plaque was also awarded to the first president, Beatrice Pitts, for her service and dedication to the auxiliary and community service.[29]

The following administrations represented years of dedication and service:

Elected Officers, 1973-75

President	: Ernestine Johnson
Vice President	: Thelma C. Moore
Recording Sec.	: Irene Day
Corres. Sec.	: Althea Cornish
Financial Sec.	: Mildred Johnson
Treasurer	: Beatrice Pitts

Elected Officers, 1975-77

President	: Carlene Gundy
Vice President	: Marie Lee
Recording Sec.	: Thelma C. Moore
Financial Sec.	: Buena Prettyman
Corres. Sec.	: Ernestine Johnson
Treasurer	: Beatrice Pitts

Elected Officers, 1977-79

President	: Mildred Johnson
Vice President	: Sara Howell
Recording Sec.	: Claudine Snowden
Corres. Sec.	: Pattine Jowers
Financial Sec.	: Thelma C. Moore
Treasurer	: Beatrice Pitts[30]

Elected Officers, 1979-81

President	: Carlene Gundy
Vice President	: Claudine Snowden
Recording Sec.	: Althea Cornish
Corres. Sec.	: Beatrice Pitts
Financial Sec.	: Irene Dodson
Treasurer	: Buena Prettyman

Elected Officers, 1981-85

President	: Sara Howell
Vice President	: Claudine Snowden
Recording Sec.	: Althea Cornish
Corres. Sec.	: Beatrice Pitts
Financial Sec.	: Sara Nix
Treasurer	: Buena Prettyman

Elected Officers, 1985-86

President	: Claudine Snowden
Vice President	: Evaline Henderson
Recording Sec.	: Althea Cornish
Corres. Sec.	: Catherine Brown
Financial Sec.	: Sara Nix
Treasurer	: Buena Prettyman

During its 27-year period of service to the community the Baltimore Auxiliary managed to initiate luncheon and seminar programs (1973-75); visitation to the Children's Ward in the local hospital, and to actively participate in National Convention and District meetings of the Frontiers (1975-77); as well as to hold active membership in the Vitiligo Foundation, Sickle Cell Anemia, United Negro College Fund, Salvation Army, Miss Santa Claus, NAACP, churches of all denominations, and local hospitals.[32]

The service of the Baltimore chapter of the Frontiers Auxiliary helped, over the years, the City of Baltimore, Maryland to become a better place to live for those who would ordinarily not have a chance in a complex urban setting, especially those who were Black and poor.

ANNAPOLIS, MARYLAND

The Annapolis Chapter was founded on January 10, 1960. Its first president was Mrs. Rose S. Wiseman who set off a spark for community involvement and participation.

At the center of its activities the Chapter was involved, since 1960, in activities like the Bywater Housing Development Tutoring Project, a grass-root support program which made a difference in the lives of the needy; and the Reading is Fundamental Project with grades 3-5 in the Bywater area.[33]

In its 1985-86 report there were 12 active members. Their enthusiasm took them to special meetings on topics which generated some concern and activity in their program development. Meeting on the topic "Hypertension and Blacks" with Dr. Elijah Saunders; and the "Status of Education in Anne Arundel County" with Dr. Robert Rice, Superintendent of Schools, sparked enthusiasm.[34]

Past historian, Yokette Irene Mills, was very helpful in providing information on the club. For example, one activity in 1985-86 that highlighted the character and hard work of the club, was their gift-giving project to the Arundel Lodge, a half-way home for former mental patients. Other worthy projects were insightful: a monetary award to the Parole Health Center "a community-run organization caring for the health needs of children and adults;" a tuition contribution for a particular needy student whose psychological and educational needs were being met at the Key School (a private institution); subscribed life members to the NAACP and the Banneker-Douglas Museum; an active participant, as a club, in the voting process of the County School Board Nominating Convention which recommended names of board members to the governor; and general community service was given when any special need was detected. The stamina of the Annapolis Club was out in the forefront in community service and service to mankind in general.

HOUSTON, TEXAS

When A. J. Dickerson and his wife Sara W. moved to Houston, Texas in August 1962, their focus on community involvement immediately took form. A. J. quickly got involved in the waning Frontiers Chapter there, which was inactive, and took steps to revitalize the organization. Sara Dickerson, as a means of support for her husband and the organization, organized Houston's first Frontiers Auxiliary (which also included unmarried daughters of Frontiers' members and widows of members).[35]

Before moving to Houston from Mobile, it was Sara Dickerson's insightful steps of encouragement and action which caused her husband and a group of men, who she recommended to the Frontiers' National Office, to start the first Frontiers Club in that town. It was also this same enthusiasm and skill which helped her to get moving on an auxiliary in Houston.

Sara became the first president elect of the Houston, Texas auxiliary. Concern for community development and social progress for Blacks vibrated her leadership and much was accomplished.[36]

In a local Houston newspaper, which captioned an impressive picture of Sara Dickerson, it gave recognition to the local auxiliary for opening a Patient's Library at Riverside General Hospital, Houston, Texas. An extraordinary ceremony took place. The local chapter received total community recognition and respect and began a tradition of public service.

SPRINGFIELD, OHIO

The Springfield Auxiliary was formed in June 1969 and chartered in November of that same year. At that time only wives and widows of Frontiers men were financial (regular dues givers). In 1985 unmarried daughters of financial Frontiersmen were allowed to join. Their community service activity focused around fund raising each year. All of the money raised was put into local community projects which benefitted the needy. They represented the highest principles of the Frontiers' service through giving.[37]

NEWARK, NEW JERSEY

The Yokettes of Newark were first organized on January 21, 1971. The Yokefellows presented them with an official charter on that same date. Official installation by Ernestine "Toots" Johnson came in June 1971 and the first meeting came in November 1971. There were 19 original members who gathered at the Owl Club, Newark, New Jersey and elected Barbara Derricote as the first president of the auxiliary. The group included (chartered members): Mary Ashby, Dorothy Barcliff, Barbara Derricote, Pauline Eastman, Ruth Edwards, Mae Hughes, Louise M. Jackson, Mary Johnson, Myrtle Jones, Irene King, Mae LeEtta Labega, May Ellen Moore, Lena Snead, Larrie Stalks, Madelyn Stanley, Jean S. Steirin, Vera Stewart, Dorothy Strickland, and Marjorie Van Dyke.[38]

In the strongest spirit of servitude to organizational and community needs the Newark Yokettes supported their Frontiers counterpart in the latter's many activities. They served as ushers and hostesses at the Frontiers Annual Awards Breakfast (by) selling tickets, ads and helping in fund raising activities to support the community needy.

As a program focus, the general activity of the Newark Club centered around raising money to support the Vitiligo Project; the Newark Girls and

80

Boys Clubs; scholarships for school to deserving youngsters; the Fresh Air Fund; needy families during the holidays; the Senior Citizens' Program; the Urban League of Essex County and the Urban League Guild; and finally, UNICEF.[39]

As of 1986 the Newark Auxiliary claimed 24 members and an active program in community service.

BRICKS TRI-COUNTY

Organized on October 24, 1972 in Enfield, North Carolina, after being sent informational notes on the purpose and structure of the Frontiers Auxiliary, the Bricks Tri-County chapter spread its new wings and called out to women of strong community service for membership. Yokette Ernestine Johnson, International Secretary, was the contact person for that first meeting. Mrs. Cleo W. Turner served as chairperson and she generated strong enthusiasm and energy.[40] After becoming an auxiliary, the following officers were elected:

President	: Cleo W. Turner
Vice President	: Janet W. Williams
Recording Sec.	: Martha S. Cooper
Corres. Sec.	: Pricilla S. Bias
Treasurer	: Lillie B. Cofield
Reporter	: Mary T. Battle

"Other charter members were Sylvia Cofield, Llana Joyner, Ione N. Knight, Rebecca T. Rogers, and Frankie Young."[41]

Detailed "housework" began during the first meetings. Joining fee was set at $5 and annual dues at $10. These funds were used to support both the national program efforts, and local community projects related to needy citizens. It was officially chartered on April 13, 1973, with a strong urge to help needy people in the local communities. The chapter grew in size and responsibility. Mrs. Cleo Turner added support to the organization by being elected as the auxiliary's International Secretary at the July 1973 National Convention held in Harrisburg, Pennsylvania.[42]

Over the years the leadership ability produced by the Bricks Tri-County Auxiliary clearly magnified on the national level. At the national level Yokette Cleo W. Turner served as recording secretary, financial secretary, vice president, and president. Yokette Frankie Young has served as corresponding secretary and a member of several national committees.[43]

The local auxiliary's past presidents were Cleo W. Turner, Frankie Young, Janet W. Williams, Martha S. Cooper, and Marjorie J. Whitaker.[44]

Leadership in any organization was produced because of those who were willing to work hard for successful programs. In the case of the Frontiers' auxiliary those programs always tend to be programs of service to mankind, especially toward the depraved and downtrodden. The Bricks Tri-County chapter showed its concern, over the years, by contributing to and participating in local Health Fairs, also donating a Sickle Cell Detective kit at one of the fairs. It made "Ditty Bags" for distribution to local rest homes for the elderly, and paid membership dues and taxes for two incapacitated members for several years. Through their fund raising activities the following organizations and projects received financial contributions: Halifax County Special Olympics; American Red Cross: Eastern NC Sickle Cell Foundation; Kidney Foundation; NC Burn Center; Life Membership in NAACP; NC Symphony; Area Rescue Squads; Enfield Nutrition Site (Meals on wheels); the Central Orphanage; the Cancer Society; Hospice; the John L. Joyner Scholarship Fund; the G. T. Young Scholarship Fund; Tornado Victims; and the Northwest and Southwest High Schools' special projects, "Time for Learning" and band uniforms.[45]

The deeds of this area chapter clearly upheld the image and profile of the Frontiers. It continues to train leaders and to center its focus on community service.

DECATUR, ILLINOIS

The Decatur Auxiliary was organized on May 13, 1974. Their criteria for membership: "any woman whose husband was a member of the Yokefellows, a Frontiersman's natural daughter after reaching the age of 21 years, and those of good moral character and civic mindedness."[46]

The first organization meeting was held at the Ambassador Motel in Decatur. From that date scheduled meetings were arranged for the second Saturday of each month at the Frontier Community House. Planning for community service activities focused on: giving food baskets to needy families at Christmas; dressing dolls for the Salvation Army for gifts to needy youngsters; operation of a clothing room in The Frontiers House (clothing was free); birthday parties at the Monroe House, a nursing facility, twice a month over a ten-year period; donated funds to Sickle Cell Unit in Decatur; donated toys to the Longview Day Care Center; sent a child to Chicago for a hair transplant after a severe burn injury; and finally, had a display for the Vitiligo Foundation (The Frontiers' special project).[47] The spirit of this very active

82

group of human service carries on and once again highlights the vision of Black women who believe in volunteerism and service to the needy.

SPRINGFIELD, ILLINOIS

The Springfield, Illinois Club of Frontiers International Women's Auxiliary was organized in January 1978. The underlying motivation came from the wives and friends of the Frontiers', they observed and believed that they could be of support to the men in the areas of community service and general contribution to the human needs of the local community.

Yokette Francine Freeman, National President in 1978, went to Springfield, Illinois and gave her assistance in organizing the local auxiliary chapter. The chapter only needed a small push on structural issue and was able to get off to a good start.[48]

The ladies of Springfield received their charter on March 28, 1978. The 16 members decided to pinpoint how they could be of service to their community. They began by making Nursing Homes, and Homes for Battered Wives their main projects. Fund raising for scholarships for needy students also became a concern.[49]

The club seemed very proud of one of its members, Yokette Mary Dickerson, for writing a prayer which was submitted to the National Convention and was accepted as a club prayer.[50] The special significance of this was the deep-rooted faith in God as a motivator, in spirit, in human affairs, especially in helping those who were willing to work, voluntarily, to meet the needs of the less fortunate among them. This was particularly significant because much of the white American attitude, in the 20th Century especially, leaned toward indicting all Black women as receivers from government and white philanthropic support; and not sound volunteers who help themselves by helping others without expecting pay or public recognition.

Since the Springfield club was organized, there have been four presidents: Yokettes Dorothy E. Smith, Georgia Hale, Martha Lambert, and Veronica Cook.[51] The torch of their spirit goes marching on doing good in community life.

WILLIAMSBURG, VIRGINIA

The Williamsburg, Virginia club began on February 25, 1982 in the home of Yokette Chestina Fallen. There were 18 chartered members.52 The charter became official on Saturday, April 24, 1982 during the Spring Conference of the Frontiers International. Club officers were installed and members received their pins indicating official membership.[53]

The first set of officers elected to office were:

President	: Chestina Fallen
Vice-President	: Florine Brown
Secretary	: Edna Parker
Treasurer	: Frances Howlette
Chaplain	: Virginia Johnson
Reporter	: Nancy James

Present members elected to office are:

President	: Dorothy Purnell
Vice-President	: Nancy James
Secretary	: Olivia Crump
Treasurer	: Josephine Hargis
Chaplain	: Beatrice Kenner[54]

TALLAHASSEE, FLORIDA

The Tallahassee Auxiliary Area Club began on May 8, 1982 in Tallahassee, Florida, when it also received its charter. Officers were elected and installed by Yokette A. E. Martin with a beginning membership of 15 ladies. Officers elected were:

President	: Janis Johnson
1st Vice Pres.	: Inell Ross
2nd Vice Pres.	: Annie B. Nelson
Secretary	: Doris Clack
Asst. Sec.	: Irene Perry
Treasurer	: Dr. Evelyn Mann
Chaplain	: Connie Lang

Dr. Evelyn Martin was appointed District Director in 1984, a fact in which the club felt very proud. Even though they have only been around a

84

few years, the club established its priorities in community service to the needy, and is continually building an image of service and dedication to directing a more functional and productive citizenry.[55]

LITTLE ROCK, ARKANSAS

The Little Rock, Arkansas Auxiliary began on October 9, 1983 through the initiatives of A. J. Dickerson of Houston, Texas, and H. R. Jones. It was a cool, fall, Sunday evening when a group of men and women met in the Freedom Life Insurance office to hear about Frontiers International They discussed organization, purpose and even the national project, Vitiligo. In fact, it was the Vitiligo disease (pigmentation leaving the skin, causing a pure white look, often spotted) which became the motivating factor in starting the auxiliary. A certain Brenda Bland (not clear from the information sent that she might have been an organizing member) confronted Yokefellow H. R. Jones in an attempt to find out about Vitiligo since she heard the Frontiers International had a special fund raising effort, nationally, for the disease. Jones, in turn, contacted District Director, Yokefellow A. J. Dickerson and a meeting between themselves and interested women constituted the first organizational auxiliary effort.[56]

At that first meeting Bettye W. Jeffries was appointed acting coordinator for the Auxiliary. A second meeting took place on November 6, 1983 to further discuss organization and Vitiligo. It was on January 15, 1984 that permanent officers were elected and installed. They were:

President	: Bettye W. Jeffries
Vice president	: Icerine Hunter
2nd Vice Pres.	: Janaytha Perry
Recording Sec.	: Essie M. Gray
Assistant	
Recording Sec.	: Jacklin Randall
Corres. Sec.	: Diane Nelson
Financial Sec.	: Linda Rainey
Treasurer	: Celestral West
Sgt.-at-Arms	: Alline Linzy
Chaplain	: Dorothy Tate
Trustee, 1 Yr.	: Amanda Coleman
Trustee, 2 Yr.	: Alline Linzy
Trustee, 3 Yr.	: Bernie Scott[57]

The Little Rock Auxiliary was officially chartered on February 13, 1984 and an installation banquet was held on March 17, 1984. Sara Dickerson of Houston, Texas, installed the officers, and A. J. Dickerson presented the Club with its charter, along with national Vice president of the Frontiers International Dale G. Lee.

The newly formed Auxiliary established as its major project, Vitiligo. It donated $1500 to the Vitiligo Research Foundation. However, other projects related to community development were quickly supported. Contributions, for example, were given to the United Negro College Fund; the Arkansas Baptist College; the Stepping Stone Agency, an organization for run-away youth; and to nursing home patients. The club also sponsored trips to Houston, Texas for nine Vitiligo patients to receive special medical attention. The primary source of financial support, to carry on the above service projects, came from annual fruit sales and the sale of Frontiers fruit cake.[58]

Service to community needs and to those persons in need have engulfed the pride and work of the Little Rock Auxiliary. It continues to be of service to its local community life, and a direct source of pride to the Frontiers organization.

CANTON, OHIO

In a sponsored cotillion for high school coeds, held Saturday, August 23, 1975, there appeared in the program magazine the following list of officers and members of the Canton Auxiliary:

President	: Lorene Pollard
Vice President	: Nadine McAlwain
Recording Sec.	: Rickie Martin
Corres. Sec.	: Ella Green
Treasurer	: Willie Andrews
Historian	: Mary Curtis
Chaplain	: Margaret McCullough
Members	: Ruby Brogdon
	Norma Ford
	Essie Gilmore
	Sheila Harris
	Jo Anne Motley
	Juanita Powe
	Geri Radcliffe
	Chleyon Thomas
	Margaret Whitfield
	Juanita Young[59]

86

In a special one-page report submitted by Yokette Jo Anne Motley, president in 1986, she signed over the title "Women's Auxiliary of the Stark County Frontiers," indicated that as of June 21, 1986, 13 cotillions had been held by the Canton Club. As she put it, it was the way of giving a purpose for the cotillions, "the cotillion helps to inspire, encourage and give recognition to outstanding young ladies of Afro-American descent."[60]

The Canton Club has, over the years of cotillion sponsorship awarded $20,500 in scholarships to deserving young women who were debutantes in the affair each year. It had the privilege of working with more than 270 young women over the course of 14 years.[61]

In the way of public achievement and recognition, the club produced two former debutantes who became "Black Football Hall of Fame Queens" (Canton is the home of the National Football League's Hall of Fame Museum). The 1985 Hall of Fame Queen, Therlanda Whitfield, was the daughter of Yokefellow and Yokette Leroy Whitfield.

The second debutante who took part in Hall of Fame activity was a part of the Hall of Fame Court which escorted Enshrinee "Willie Lanier."[62]

AKRON, OHIO

In an article which appeared in a local newspaper (The Reporter), January 24-31, 1976, pictures and names appeared of the Akron Auxiliary's newly installed officers. They were:

President	: Clarisse Keyes	
Vice President	: Bevy Lewis	
Parliamentarian	: Bernice Conley	
Recording Sec.	: Maggie Pool	
Treasurer	: Dorothy Welch	
Corres. Sec.	: Dorothea Moore	
Historian	: Sarah Brown	
Chaplain	: Gloria Peavy	
Members	Mildred Cummings	
	Joyce Jackson	
	Ada Mitchell	
	Esther Spruill	
	Muriel Walker	

MILWAUKEE, WISCONSIN

The Auxiliary Club of Milwaukee, Wisconsin received its charter on May 15, 1978. Officers elected and installed were:

President	: Gwen Jackson
Secretary	: Sandra Henderson
Treasurer	: Josephine Green
Members	: Paris Madison
	Geraldine Goens
	Carolyn Belton
	Birdie Hobson
	Evelyn Cleveland[63]

The first activity of the club was to assist the Milwaukee Frontiers in its 15th Annual Golf Tournament, a fund raising activity. Other projects of community interest were teen pregnancy, redirecting "at-risk" children, and senior citizens' concerns. The spirit of giving helped to meet their challenges and concerns.

SAGINAW, MICHIGAN

Each year the Saginaw Auxiliary supports the Annual Project Banquet with the local Frontiers. They also jointly support the annual Christmas Shopping Spree in December. These are fund raising activities which support community projects for the needy. Other activities include the Senior Citizens of Community Villages, Saginaw Battered Women's Home, Community Education Department of Science, Tri-City Links Beautillion Scholarship Fund, Phi Delta Kappa Youth Scholarship Fund, Good Neighbors Mission, United Negro College Fund, and the Opportunities Industrialization Centers. [64]

Juanita Fox, as Auxiliary President, had done an excellent job in encouraging fund raising activities which support the programs listed above. The principles of the Frontiers again unfold on red carpet.

AN OVERVIEW

It would take more than public praise to meet the standards of volunteerism. The hard work and "callbeyond-duty" efforts of those Black women in American cities who called themselves Yokettes and organized under Frontiers International Auxiliaries, and who tried to help the less fortunate without reward, were the shining stars of granddaughters and great-granddaughters of American slaves. They became educated, became wives and sisters and mothers and are pouring out good will to those in the Black and other minority communities who were not able to advance as far as they.

In summary, the Yokettes of the Frontiers can be compared to an experience that Mary McLeod Bethune had in 1934 when she was invited to the White House to discuss the National Youth Administration program with President Franklin Delano Roosevelt. She effectively pleaded the case for Black youth which impressed the President immensely. In another meeting Roosevelt chose Mrs. Bethune to represent Black youth as a special NYA advisor. He was quoted as saying, referring to the volunteer deeds of Mary Bethune, "Mrs. Bethune is a great woman. I believe in her. She has her feet on the ground, not only on the ground, but in the plowed soil."[65] The women of the Frontiers, in comparison, are like that--their feet planted solidly in commitment to community service, so much so that their feet are "plowed in the soil" until the needs of the poor, the uneducated, the hungry, the elderly, and the handicapped are met.

NOTES

[1]Stephen Henderson, <u>Understanding The New Black Poetry</u> (N.Y.: William Morrow & Co., Inc., 1973) pp. 126-127.

[2]Margaret Hennig and Anne Jardin (N.Y.: Pocket Books, 1978), p. 188.

[3]Toni Cade, ed., <u>The Black Woman</u> (N.Y.: Signet Books, 1970), p. 87.

[4]<u>The Coordinating Council, Women's Auxiliaries of the Frontiers International Constitution</u> (Revised 1976), p. 3.

[5]Ibid.

[6]Ibid.

[7]Ibid, p. 4.

[8]Ibid.

[9]Ibid, p. 12.

[10]An undated listing, presumably written and dated around 1978-79.

[11]An undated statement on Sara Dickerson, presumably written and dated around 1977.

[12]Alma J. Fletcher, President of Philadelphia Auxiliary, a letter dated October 8, 1986.

[13-20]Ibid.

[21]Claudine Snowden, President of Baltimore Auxiliary, a letter dated October 14, 1986.

[22]Claudine Snowden, undated newspaper clipping.

[23]Ibid.

[24]Report on elected officials,1986.

[25-32]Ibid.

[33]Mary C. Brown, President of Annapolis, Md.,
Auxiliary, letter dated October 22, 1986.

[34]Ibid.

[35]Sara Dickerson, historical statement, Houston, Texas,
1986.

[36]Ibid.

[37]Joyce Isley, President, Springfield, Ohio Auxiliary,
a letter dated October 10, 1986.

[38]Odessa Fountain, President, Newark, N.J. Auxiliary,
statement dated February 29, 1987.

[39]Ibid.

[40]Marjorie Whitaker, President, Bricks Tri-County
Auxiliary, statement dated February 3, 1987.

[41-45]Ibid.

[46]Essie Lee Travis, President; and Goldie L. Kennedy,
Secretary, Decatur, Ill., statement dated October 10, 1986.

[47]Ibid.

[48]Dorothy E. Smith, past President of Springfield,
Ill., statement dated October 15, 1986.

[49-51]Ibid.

[52]Josephine Hargis, Treasurer, Williamsburg, Va.
Chapter of Auxiliary, statement dated April 1987.

[53]Ibid.

[54]Ibid.

[55]Annie B. Nelson, President, Tallahassee, Fla.
Auxiliary, letter dated October 11, 1986.

[56]Bettye W. Jeffries, President, Little Rock, Ark.,
statement dated October 1986.

[57]Ibid.

[58]Ibid.

[59]Canton, Ohio 1975 program magazine.

[60]JoAnne Motley, Canton, Ohio, statement dated July 9,
1986.

[61]Ibid.

[62]Ibid.

[63]Frontiersman newsletter, vol. 15, number 2, April,
May, June 1978, p. 4, col. I

[64]Armell G. Woods, Saginaw Mich., statement dated July
1986.

[65]Jesse Walter Dees, Jr., The College Built on Prayer:
Mary McLeod Bethune (N.Y.: Ganis and Harris, 1953), p. 37.

CHAPTER VII

"A FISH IN THE SEA"

There are many Black public service organizations which are dedicated to community service in urban America. They range from fraternities /sororities to government-oriented agencies. Each has historically proven its worth as a functionary component of a strong desire to improve the quality of life for the average Black American. From fund raising to individual contributions, the unselfish vision of a number of well-meaning people has contributed to a number of projects (educational scholarships, food supply projects, health and disease control and other concerns) and have, as a result, supported the notion that there was/is a strong effort being made by Black citizens to initiae self-help and not depend on the broader White community for total support.

Black organizations and White organizations, structurally, were alike on the surface, but there were vast differences underneath when considering organizational focus, long-range/short-range goals, and overall group philosophy. The Frontiers International Incorporated is one of those unique Black organizations, different from the other Black structural forms, but strongly supportive of the idea of service to the needy. In order to properly highlight the contributions of the Frontiers, focus on the structure, and purpose of Black organizations should be given attention. Without their existence in the 20th Century American scene, the Black community would be much further behind socially. Their existence tended to collaborate one another, so that, in the final analysis, organizations like the Frontiers were actually strengthened by the presence of other Black groups.

The nature, goal or purpose of any organization was given originally by its founders. In like turn, persons who had the vision and incentive to put together an organizational structure were motivated by social needs of the larger society.[1] In the case of those Black organizations which emerged at the beginning of the 20th Century the urgent social needs of Black communities across America responded to their program formats for service and duty. Their founders were Black men (e.g., Nimrod Allen, founder of the Frontiers) and women who had social concerns for their local communities and for the uplift of Black Americans in general.

One of the areas, based on program activities, which is not often considered, is the fact that an organization like the Frontiers International has gained its strength as a service group due to the fact that there were other Black organizations contributing in the same social arena. This is to say that the strength of any organization, in carrying out its social duties, gains strength and is recognized more in the public eye, when there are other similar organizations performing cooperatively, the same or similar social functions. Raising scholarship money, for example, for Black young people to attend college, has not only been a function for a number of Frontiers' clubs around the country, but Black fraternities and sororities, various Black union and private groups have also performed the same deeds. Their activities, in this regard, tended to complement one another as opposed to competing. This practice has tended to make the Frontiers an even strongerand more effective organization. In a recent study on interorganizational relationships, in order to support the above point, "All organizations have relationships with other organizations. . .Organizations use other organizations of the same type both for comparison purposes and as a source of new ideas."[2]

The very strength and heart of the Frontiers International Inc. historically was made up of Black men functioning at local club levels. Men from the business, educational, and professional world were members. They were persons who tended to have a strong commitment to service and a sense for a better way of life for the less fortunate. Its members (i.e., including the Women's Auxiliaries) were often members of other non-profit service organizations such as the YMCA, YWCA, scholarship concerns, United Way, NAACP, Urban League, various fraternities and sororities, and the Big Brother and Big Sister Programs.

In the way of being supportive to the development of the Frontiers International, and how it gained its strength from the existence of other Black organizations, the following information will focus on the structure and policy of a few groups.

Since the period of Reconstruction in America, a number of Black organizations were established to focus on the economic and social needs of the Black community. A listing of organizations and dates, as follows, would be appropriate to show the large number of men and women in the Black community who have, since the turn of the century, been dedicated to public service (in alphabetical order):

Alpha Kappa Alpha Sorority	-	1908
Alpha Kappa Mu Honor Society	-	1937
Alpha Phi Alpha Fraternity, Inc.	-	1906

American Teachers Association   -
      Ancient and Accepted Scottish
      Rite Masons   -   1864
Ancient Egyptian Arabic Order,
      Nobles of the Mystic Shrine-
Benevolent Protective Order
      of Reindeer   -   1923
Bible Way, Church of Our Lord
      Jesus World Wide, Inc.   -   1957
Central Intercollegiate
      Athletic Association   -
Chi Delta Mu Fraternity   -   1913
Chi Eta Phi Sorority   -   1932
Drifters, Inc.   -
Eta Phi Beta Sorority, Inc.   -
*Frontiers International   -   1936
Gamma Phi Delta Sorority   -   1940
Girl Friends, Inc.   -
Grand Temple Daughters   -   1902
Grand United Order of Odd Fellows
Imperial Court, Daughters of Isis -   1910
Improved Benevolent
      Protective Order of
      Elks of the World   -   1898
International Conference
      of Grand Chapters Order
      of the Eastern Star   -   1907
Jack and Jill of America, Inc.   -
Kappa Alpha Psi Fraternity   -   1911
Knights of Peter Claver   -   1909
Lambda Kappa Mu Sorority, Inc. -   1937
Links, Inc.   -   1946
National Alumni Council of
      The United Negro College
      Fund   -
National Association of
      Barristers' Wives   -   1949
National Association of
      College Deans and
Registrars   -   1926
National Association of
      Colored Women's Clubs, Inc.

National Association of
  Fashion and Accessory
  Designers, Inc.
	-	1950

National Association of Market Developers	-	1953
National Association of Ministers' Wives	-	1941

National Association of Negro
  Business and Professional
  Women's Clubs
	-	1935

National Association of Negro Musicians	-	1919
National Association of Real Estate Brokers	-	
National Bankers Association	-	1926
National Bar Association	-	1925
National Beauty Culturists League	-	1919
National Business League	-	1900
National Conference of Artists	-	1959
National Convention of Gospel Choirs and Choruses	-	1932
National Council of Negro Women	-	1935
National Dental Association	-	1913
National Epicureans	-	1951
National Funeral Directors and Morticians Association	-	
National Grand Chapter of the Eastern Star	-	
National Housewives' League of America	-	
National Insurance Association	-	1921
National Medical Association	-	1895
National Newspaper Publishers Association	-	1940
National Technical Association	-	1926
National United Church Ushers Association of America	-	1919
Nationwide Hotel-Motel Association	-	
Omega Psi Phi Fraternity	-	1911
Phi Beta Sigma Fraternity	-	1914
Tau Gamma Delta Sorority	-	1942
United Mortgage Bankers of America, Inc.	-	

Women's Auxiliary to the
    Benevolent Protective
    Order of Reindeer   -
Women's Auxiliary to the National
    Medical Association   -   3

Listing the Black organizations above was not done to make a comparison between those groups doing social service in the Black community, rather it merely highlighted the fact that their activity was complimentary to the strength and function of the Frontiers. A few descriptions of select organizations, emphasizing their philosophy and purpose, would be appropriate.

The National Council of Negro Women, for example, founded in 1935, by the distinguished educator, Mary McLeod Bethune, along with 35 eminent women, gathered together to map out a program for united planning and concerted action by various Negro women's organizations, and establish an "organization which would serve as a kind of clearing house for the activities of one million women." It was primarily concerned about "the economic, social, cultural and educational welfare of Negro women in particular."[4]

One of the best descriptions of Black fraternity and sorority life in America was given by the writer, Paula Giddings. She suggested that a sorority like Delta Sigma Theta, for example, could be "better understood when seen in the light of the principles that govern social movement organizations. . . they must be able to adapt to changing environments: in this case, the ever changing exigencies of race relations and the attitudes toward women."[5] She also suggested that "social movement organizations are also dependent on the attitudes of the larger society toward both the movement that they represent and the organization itself."[6]

The more legitimate it (organization) is seen
in the broader society, sociologists say, the
more potential supporters became actual
supporters. The ideal condition for organizational growth is a strong sentiment base
with a low societal hostility toward the
movement and the organization. This, too,
has important implications in terms of its
public activities and the need to maintain
not only respect but a deep loyalty of the
members.[7]

Even though there have been similarities in social concerns among Black groups like the Greek sororities, fraternities and the Frontiers, there were basic differences in orientation and program. These differences tended to direct incomparable approaches to social concerns in the Black community. Fraternal organizations, for example, tended to have an exclusive or closed membership. . . .Undergraduate members must be in college. All members must be invited to join, and undergo a final selection process that includes both quantifiable criteria (for example, grade point average) and/or subjective assessments regarding achievement and character.[8]

Certainly, Black fraternities and sororities came along at a time in American history (e.g., turn of the 20th Century) when it was necessary to have such organizations with rigid internal criteria for membership. They had their place in the development of solid Black community life and continue to contribute in key areas of concern. "By 1912, there were 256,000 members in forty such organizations in the country, including the Black fraternities, Alpha Phi Alpha (1906), Kappa Alpha Psi (1911), Omega Psi Phi (1911); and the sorority Alpha Kappa Alpha (1908). Soon following was the establishment of Delta Sigma Theta (1913) and Zeta Phi Beta (1920) sororities, and Phi Beta Sigma fraternity (1914)."[9] Evident in this Greek arena was the unique paradigm of a closed, exclusive pattern of membership "and the culture of secret societies replete with rituals, oaths, and symbols. Members of all the groups had to meet particular criteria and go through novitiate periods where they were subjected to hazing and the discipline and orders of the organization. All were created out of the desire to form social bonds with likeminded students."[10]

One of the areas of credit, however, given to the secret societies called sororities/fraternities, which is somewhat unique, was the fact that in their attempt to translate "the concept of service into political activism" the sorority (e.g., Delta Sigma Theta) was not conceived to transform society but to transform the individual."[11]

The Delta's, for example, were typical in their philosophical purpose as it met the needs of the broader community. It internalized its projection of service to humanity by first committing itself to high standards among its membership, i.e. "to establish and maintain a high standard of morality and scholarship among women generally."[12]

The Alpha Kappa Alpha Sorority tended to also give a broad commitment to community life within a narrow context. Its program attempted to "discharge some of (its) responsibilities for bettering social and economic conditions in (its) expanding community."[13] Even though this notion could easily compare to the broader works of the Frontiers, as the latter group performs social commitments, only, however, with a broader contextual base in its philosophy. Not confined to secrecy and rigid entrance requirements based on sex roles and privacy social service is relegated to the problems and needs of each community across the country. The work of college fraternities and sororities, do, however, add to the incentive of organizations like the Frontiers International program because in those communities where both organizations exist there is a tendency to cooperate on common social issues. According to one source the point was made clear, "Clients of social service organizations are vitally affected by interorganizational relationships. A common practice is client referral, theoretically, if one agency is unable to provide the needed services for a particular client."[14]

The objectives and philosophy of the Zeta Phi Beta Sorority, Inc., for example, has been very supportive of the Frontiers program wherever both organizations existed in the same communities. The former's objectives were "finer womanhood, excellence in all areas of education, good human and public relations, volunteer and service projects which focused on concerns for health, education and welfare services."[15] A parent training program under what Zetas called "Operation Bootstrap" was a part of a national program effort in the same way that concerns for the Vitiligo disease was a national project for the Frontiers.

Other organizational programs outside of the fraternity/sorority structure have also been highly visible and cooperative in their social service programs. The Frontiers International has benefitted from their presence and cooperation. One such Black organization, concerned about the needs of the Black community, was the National Association of University Women. In the latter's program their outreach efforts focused on promoting the improvement of education and related educational and public pursuits. From its inception in 1974, it made a special effort, as a part of its charter, "to cooperate with other groups, associations, public or private agencies which may be concerned with community problems, cultural interests, educational and world problems" and "to cooperate with and assist other organizations, institutions, agencies and bodies both public and private, on a national, sectional and local level in promoting academic and intellectual attainment. . . ."[16] The Frontiers, as well as other service organizations benefitted from the program support of the NAUW.

Another supportive Black organization, with a unique function, was the North Carolina Mutual and Provident Association. Seven Black men met on an October evening, 1898, in Durham, North Carolina and organized around the purpose "to aid Negro families in distress," and established the motto "Merciful to All."[17] Similar to the pursuits of Nimrod Allen and his cohorts of the Frontiers International, the North Carolina Mutual and Provident Association took up the task to the "relief of widows and orphans, of the sick and of those injured by accident, and the burial of the dead, and . . . a certain per centum of the proceeds, to be fixed by the board of directors, shall be turned over to the Colored Asylum at Oxford, North Carolina."[18] How many Yokefellows of the Frontiers worked for or were associated with the North Carolina Mutual program? An answer to this question could only add to the strength and cooperation of Black men with a mission of service to community life. "Far from being just an economic institution, the Mutual stood as a expression of Afro-American thought centering on the doctrine of selfhelp and racial solidarity."[19] The proclamation for self-help by the North Carolina Mutual was similar to the Frontiers: "We as a race have reached the point where we must try to turn up something for ourselves. . . . Our every departure into business is a sign that we are. . . eager to go from infancy to manhood."[20]

People who are willing to dedicate their time and energy to human service are unique, but are also those persons who, after joining a service organization, adapt quickly to its program and philosophy. "Human beings participate in formal groups in terms of identities that they adopt, take over, move into, or occupy by virtue of participating in that group."[21]

If there can be any sense of comparison of the Frontiers International with any other Black service organization, it would be in how programs function on a national scale. The history of the Frontiers, for example, was the composite history of each of its individual clubs. Even though there might have been similar concerns in those towns or cities where chapters were located, how they approached problems or establish programs was unique to the character and vision of each group. This was consistent with studies that have been done on how organizations function. "Decisions are. . . based on tradition and precedent, as well as the organization's relationships with its environment."[22] According to two organizational experts, Burrell and Morgan, "voluntarism sees humans as totally autonomous and free willed, while determinism sees people as totally controlled by the situation or environment in which they are located. The analysis here leans toward the determinist perspective without embracing it totally."[23]

The Frontiers, as well as other organizations, are governed by a national format (i.e., a written set of principles) which focus a direction of activity at local levels. The Frontiers tended to part from other Black organizations in that most of what it did, at a functional level, was focused around the communities where chapters were located. Each club was not mandated to report to a national office or feel inhibited in experimenting with creative social activity. There was, however, a national code of conduct and a strong sense of national loyalty.

In looking at the historical development of organizations like the Frontiers one cannot deny the profound impact of the old "Negro lodges" which transcended out of the 19th century arena in America. Prior to the first World War (around 1937) "the total membership in 60-odd Negro societies is approximately 2,500,000 and the property they own is probably in the neighborhood of $20,000,000, built on catechistic statements and high moral principles."

As early as 1693, during the period of slavery, Cotton Mather (noted White clergyman) wrote "Rules for the Society of Negroes." "Every Sunday evening the slaves were allowed to assemble and pray together by turns. There was ceremony and dim outlines of a Grand United Order back of these gatherings."[24] Even though this assemblage did not represent the free expression by free citizens in organizational structure, it did represent an early attempt by Blacks to help one another on the slave plantation to survive.

In the antebellum period, around 1847, "pious souls" organized the Independent Order of Good Samaritans and the Daughters of Samaria. Its purpose was "to spread the cause of temperance among the colored"[25] people. To a limited degree it was a functionary group, considering the stresses and limitation of the slavery structure. They did exercise some form of internal control and self-help. Black organizations, during this time period, were without question, affected by racial division and set a precedent for later generations of Black organizations. These early groups fell under the "Colored Masons" movement. They had names like Crystal Fount, Rose of Sharon, Lily of the Valley, Good Intent, Ark of Safety, Neversink, Hand in Hand, Gassaway, Rising Star of the East, and Mt. Pisgah. Their importance to "Negro life" was not so much that they had restrictions and the watchful eye of white slaves, but that they existed at all with members eagerly helping the needy amongst them. Their presence set a precedent for organizations like the Frontiers because they performed, in spite of social limitations, enormous social and psychological self-help feats. In the words of a Negro Mason, during that period:

> The great truths of Masonry headed, consti-
> tute a security within an impregnable for-
> tress surrounding the human soul against
> which the weapons of evil will fall broken at
> our feet, and we are as little harmed as the
> atoms which dance in the sunbeams and nestle
> against our window panes.[26]

The Masonry and similar organizations like the Odd Fellowship tended to supply a sense of power and security[27] during a time in American history when slavery was on its final leg and Black men were searching for new identities.

The Frontiers International benefitted both in philosophical projections and psychological support as it fell back on the long tradition of non-profit Black organizations which began prior to the Emancipation Proclamation years. Those organizations which have grown up with the Frontiers continue to supplement and support the latter as it fulfills its mission of service to humanity.

NOTES

[1]Charles K. Warriner, <u>Organizations and Their Environments</u> (Conn.: Jai Press Inc., 1984), p.11

[2]Richard H. Hall, <u>Organizations: Structures and Process,</u> (N.J.: Prentice-Hall, Inc., 1982), pp.239 & 243.

[3]Roscoe C. Brown and Harry A. Ploski, <u>The Negro Almanac,</u> (N.Y.: Bellwether Publishing Co., Inc., 1967), pp. 817-819.

[4]Ibid., p.820.

[5]Paula Giddings, <u>In Search of Sisterhood: Delta Sigma Theta and the Challenge of the Black Sorority Movement,</u> (N.Y.: William Morrow and Co. Inc., 1988) p.6.

[6]Ibid.

[7]Ibid., p.7.

[8]Ibid.

[9]Ibid., p.17.

[10]Ibid.

[11]Ibid., p.21.

[12]Ibid., p.26.

[13]Loc. Cit., Brown and Ploski, p.820.

[14]Loc. Cit., Hall, p.239.

[15]A program pamphlet titled "Finer Womanhood Scholarship Awards Luncheon," Eta Omicron Zeta Chapter, Zeta Phi Beta Sorority, Inc., p.1.

[16]An organizational pamphlet (undated) describing the structure and program of the NAUW.

[17]Walter B. Weare, <u>Black Business in the New South</u>, (Chicago: University of Illinois Press, 1973), pp.29 & 31.

[18]Ibid., p.31.

[19]Ibid., p.95.

[20]Ibid., p.96.

[21]Ibid., p.38.

[22]Hall, Loc. Cit., p.38.

[23]Ibid., p.39.

[24]Ibid., p.185.

[25]Ibid.

[26]Ibid., p.187.

[27]Ibid., p.189.

CHAPTER VIII

AFRICA AND AMERICA

Just as so many native New Yorkers postpone their promised visits to the Statue of Liberty, Frontiers International has for years postponed its promised active recruitment of African and Caribbean clubs and members.

Concerning the Caribbean - On July 22, 1965 Yokefellow Vibart Tampkin, an executive member of the British Guiana branch of Frontiers International, was the main speaker at that year's International Convention which was held at New York City's Waldorf Astoria Hotel. The distinguished Yokefellow was Solicitor of the Supreme Court of British Guiana and Ambassador Designate to the United States Government.[1]

In 1964 the elected officers of the British Guiana Frontiers Club, which was organized in February 1961 and which held its meetings at the Woodbine Hotel, 41 Newmarket Street, Georgetown, British Guiana, were: Basil Bunyan, President; John Carter, Vice-President; Eric Shepherd, Secretary-Treasurer; and W. D. Wilson, Chaplain. (On May 26, 1966, British Guiana declared its independence and changed its name to Guyana.)[2]

Concerning Africa - A long list of African natives have joined the Frontiers International while they were living or studying in the United States. Among them was Nija Kwiawon Toryor of Ghan, Liberia; James Oyedukun Adeseko of Lagos, Nigeria; Dr. Emmet Dennis of Liberia; and R. Charles Onsomu of Nairobi, Kenya.[3]

The following letter from Mr. Onsomu to the International Frontiers Headquarters, written in 1976, reveals not only the cultural differences between Black America and Black Africa but shows also the scope of hopes and expectations the Frontiers International service organization arouses among the countries of Africa:

Letter From Kenya

17th January, 1976

Dear Executive Secretary:

I delightfully received and read your lucid materials the first which I replied while in Great Britain and the recent of December.

I herewith forward along with my entrance fee, anxiously awaiting your approval to enable my annual payment to reach you early enough.

Turning my eyes to the organization, I propose creation of Frontiers in Kenya will be entirely a new approach that will come up with great results in terms of its eventual prosperous importance among the communities with their full support only if they may be informed in the advertisement.

Now being in the position to serve as an affiliate Representative in this ambitious effort as to my motive to accept theresponsibility for the consequences of any decision I make prior to the margin of my being born with love of humanity, I speak to you here in a spirit of hope that with the cooperation of Frontiers deserving philanthropic certified arbiters I will commence a permanent, proper and true foundation of this peaceful land that will bring about a joint result and remain as a bilateral bridge fruitful and creative on effective growth climate in the social change and expansional capacity on the direction where not only Kenyans will benefit but East Africans as a whole.

When I made this decision I didn't desire this for my narrow self interest and left those of my fellowmen with every hope of real aspiration to encourage and maintain good relations with others by paying a price for the Club's survival in the aspect of observing how my sincere sense of moralresponsibility will have on them as to my ability to approach relationships, problems and appraise myself and my performance, honestly.

Having expounded your cherishment in the role of service and international understanding by your data indication, things are caused to happen as problems required solutions and I indeed believe that we can use this system to foster and promote black performance on the

106

continent and set a formula of how you former brothers can devote your deeper commitment in service modernizing the translation of Negro history which has been so silent almost in every field, particularly in Kenya.

Since the key to success lies within Kenyans, I introduced and conducted a Frontiers private audition inquiry persuading my friends who held a welcome home dance in my honor to make their choice and become participants rather than mere observers, and the demand they brought to my notice was "Organizing For Action." Interim branch more reflectable to pursue their attitudination towards the basic cause of doing so in Nairobi.

Others differed in expressions my unmarried mates prefer to join because of their loneliness so we claimed to join and use the club as a tool to speed our national developmental cooperation. Three vitiligo victims who lodged a complaint for poor treatment wondered if a special clinic can be established in Nairobi for the Kenyans.

One student sought more information about scholarships and pleaded his will to use the club as a trail for his higher education in an American Black university.

The married middle aged claimed for a particular place where the General Public willing to join can get information. Some expressed their feelings of so doing due to the club's general code and its privileges and extended their welcome invitation to their brothers to come and re-unite on the black soil again. The rest demanded charter membership. Most of them implored the period dues are paid to be extended, January being a month that a lot of demands to be fulfilled.

I therefore forward this in the circumstances of your proposals how Kenyans can listen to a problem and express their feelings reasonably. Finally, to achieve the appropriate successful goals will spell full responsibility of more than one person (professional expert) and long-term member to assist in ensuring that all programs and actions are undertaken with careful reverence for the needs of Frontiers initiative qualities.

When addressing a letter, quote my address and the letter to be under the care of MR. ALBERT. This results from my being away from duty caring for my mother and brother in the hospital where they are receiving treatment to the injuries they sustained following a car accident on January 1st, 1976 until my further notice.

I convey my greetings to all the member and wish them and the
club a happy and prosperous New Year.

Very truly yours,

Raphael Charles Onsomu
Sales Public Relations Assistant
P.O. Box 40254
Kenyatta Avenue
Nairobi, Kenya[4]

Beginning with the notion that somehow Black American institutions
were replicas or duplications of early African structural life was a debative
point. Africanists in America generally took a solid stand on the side of
"carry-over," i.e., that many Black American organizations and institutions
(e.g., churches) were closely related to the philosophical heritage of African
practices prior to the slavery period. There were others, however, who would
contend that Black American institutional life was a creation of the American
phenomenon and was directly affected by institutional slavery and
Americanization since 1492.

The noted African theologian, John S. Mbiti, helped us to see clearly
the distinction between traditional African structural practices and its
contemporary affects in Africa. For example, he suggested that African group
life centered around religious behavior and family life. "African peoples are
deeply religious and experience this as a religious universe. . . ."[5] In
traditional life the family is the nucleus of both individual and corporate
existence, the area where a person really experiences personal consciousness
of himself and of other members of society."[6] Clubs, fraternal organizations,
and similar groups were not historically a part of the African setting until
contemporary times, i.e., not until the post-Second- World-War period, and
even then were tinted with religious and familial undertones.

"The physical expansion of Europe into Africa," suggested Mbiti,
exposed African peoples to the change taking place elsewhere. It was in this
atmosphere of structural take-over that institutional practices from the
European-Western model, like clubs, associations, and formal groups,
emerged. However, the historical strength of family and religious practices
undergirded the psycho- logical association of membership in any group.
Mbiti made the point emphatic: "On the material or economic level, the
trend is clearly the cultivation of individual and national prosperity. But on
the emotional and psychological level, it is towards tribal solidarity and

108

foundations."[7] The onslaught of urbanization and technological growth gave, on its surface, a taste of western civilization, but the process of internal stabilization remained a mental and spiritual matter.

The profound point that Mbiti made regarding organizational structure, which intruded into the African social scene with industrialization, focused at the heart of how westernization affected the African personality. Tribal solidarity based on intricate forms of human relationships was interrupted by a new form of ethical behavior brought on by city living.

> The individualism of urban life demands its own code of behaviour. Whereas in rural life the individual is "naked" to everybody else, in the city he is a locked-up universe of his own. The concept of "neighbour" differs considerably in the two situations (i.e., tribal and city). In the city the individual is one in a loose conglomeration of men and women from different peoples and languages, races and nationalities. These are joined or related together not by bonds of blood and betrothal, but by professions, places of work, clubs, factories, associations, hobbies, trade unions, sports, political parties, church denominations and religious ties. That is where the individual now finds himself, and often his loyalties are spread over many of these affiliations.[8]

Organizational life in modern Africa, affected by western values based on individualism, acknowledged the fact that "emphasis is shifting from the 'we' of traditional corporate life to the 'I' of modern individualism."[9] Groups like the Rotary Club and the Opportunities Industrialization Centers (OIC) began to augment the natural familial practices of group dynamics. Even the size of the family shrank "from the traditional 'extended' family concept to one in which the parents and their children constituted family in the modern sense (i.e. nuclear-husband, wife and children)."[10] Even marriage contracts, in the post-Second-World-War period, became increasingly individual affairs and "the concept of two persons, rather than the concern of families and communities,"[11] became a fact of life. In the past, becoming a member of the group (primarily family and tribe) was a religious and ritualistic affair, but slowly changed to membership by a ssociation (e.g., the Rotary Club).

Adaptability from one social pattern to another in the African social fabric was intrinsically complex but extrinsically flexible. The family structure, for example, adhered to what was called a "kinship" structure (a unique pattern of extension within the group). ". . . the system (i.e., kinship) means that no one is without siblings and the mutual support and responsibility which is characteristic of relationships between siblings. . . it provides every individual with a group of 'primary' kinsmen, and that has many advantages in societies which rely upon close cooperation, as opposed to our isolating type of terminology in a society which emphasizes individuality."[12] It was not difficult, in some cases, to adapt to group structures that were social in nature outside of the family unit. Joining clubs and economic, social or political organizations could only serve as a support to an inclusive posture like kinship. Social stratification based on class and caste often became the outcome of group formation. Western influence, through colonization, affected traditional social patterns only in a political, social or economic group did not replace the traditional family group structure, it only augmented it. As Professor of International Development Vera M. Dean put it: "When European governments took over many of the political functions of the old kinship and lineage systems, they did not provide adequate substitutes for the social and economic balance, harmony, and security of the old regime. Consequently, the African still relies on the building up of personal obligations to himself through the old system of social relationships."[13] Modernization and Westernization did have its affect on 20th-Century Africa. It was unfortunate that Black American organizations did not get a foothold on the African scene in the same way as White-oriented groups, e.g., the Rotary Club.

Nnamdi Azikiwe, the first independent leader of Nigeria, West Africa, spoke of his invitation and active membership in various groups as an undergraduate and graduate student in the U. S. He was invited and became a member of the American Political Science Association, the American Society of International Law, the American Anthropological Association, the American Ethnological Society, and the Institute of Journalists. The only Black organization that had any lasting effect on "Zik" (pet name), was the Mu Chapter of the Phi Beta Sigma Fraternity at Lincoln University, Lincoln, Pennsylvania.[14]

In the same manner, Kwame Nkrumah, the first independent leader of Ghana, West Africa, like "Zik" was a member of the Phi Beta Sigma Fraternity when he was an undergraduate student at Lincoln University, Lincoln, Pennsylvania. He was impressed by its motto, "Culture for Service and Service for Humanity."[15] Neither he nor Azikiwe attempted to establish a chapter of this Black American connection in their respective countries, probably due to the fact that a secret society like a Greek fraternity would not

110

have caught on to the African psychic easily. Nkrumah became a member, during his student days in America, of the National Maritime Union and organized the African Students' Association of America and Canada. He came into contact with the Council on African Affairs, the Committee on Africa, the Committee on War and Peace Times, the Committee on African Students, the Special Research Council of the National Association for the Advancement of Colored People, and the Urban League.[16]

After looking at the small number of African young men who came to America in the post-World War I years and who joined the Frontiers International, one would wonder why the large number of Black American organizations had limited impact on African participation. None of the organizations seemed to take hold and form counterparts on the African continent, especially in Ghana and Nigeria, West Africa, where the largest contingent of African students, following Azikiwe and Nkrumah, came to America for college study. Dr. Emment Dennis, Professor at Rutgers University, New Brunswick, New Jersey, and a member of the Frontiers International, from Liberia, West Africa, gave an excellent account of the African connection with organizations like the Frontiers.

Dr. Dennis joined the Frontiers International around 1973. He was influenced by Black American friends that he associated with and from the Frontiers historical perspectives which focused on philanthropic and nationalistic concerns.[17] Even though he had some interests, as probably many Africans had when associating with Black organizations, the rigid schedule of work and study did not allow him to carry his interests out on returning to Liberia and establishing a chapter there.

"In Liberia," suggested Dennis, "as with most countries in Africa where similar social organizations have been established, Rotary, for example, had a tremendous foundation, almost religious in nature. We may have been dealing in the past with a segregated club, which Frontiers virtually copied, in terms of its own ideals and direction. Perhaps in the U. S. today Rotary might still be a predominantly Caucasian organization, but this is not true for Rotary International, which I personally consider to be the major competitor of Frontiers International. Rotary has a stronghold in Liberia, and many other African countries where the Blacks in these places don't know Rotary's history or appreciate the historical perspective of Rotary and the prejudice that existed in it."[18] In Africa, Rotary is run by Blacks who comprise its membership and have little knowledge of the limited vision on the question of race in the American clubs. Rotary was/is the major competitor for the Frontiers in Africa because Africans were more exposed to predominantly white social organizations as students in America. However, there were specific reasons why Africans, who came to America during the post-World

111

War II years, gravitated to organizations like the Rotary and escaped association with Black clubs like the Frontiers where they should have "made their home."

There were specific reasons why Rotary was able to have an impact on the African continent and the Frontiers did not:

1. During the post-African independence period, around the 1950's and 1960's, when countries like Ghana (under Kwame Nkrumah), and Nigeria (under Nnamdi Azikiwe), sent a large number of students to the African Centers at Lincoln University, Pennsylvania and Harvard University, Massachusetts, they made contact with organizations like the Rotary through strong invitation and recruitment efforts.

2. The philosophy of the Rotary did not have written language of racial exclusion and appealed to young Africans seeking association with an organization that seemed to have economic and international clout.

3. Africans in the U. S. joined the Rotary Club, as opposed to seeking out Black organizations like the Frontiers, and returned to their homes in Africa with the intent of establishing chapters.

4. The public relations aspect of the Frontiers, historically, did not match the program of the Rotary, therefore, the latter put more effort and had more re-sources to influence African membership and participation.

5. Even though the Frontiers had similar principles when compared to the Rotary, and were pinpointing the needs of the Black community in America directly, it did not focus much effort on attracting Africans.

6. The Rotary Club probably had a better public relations system than other organizations in America. The Frontiers were no match.

7. The reason for the founding of the Frontiers was because Rotary, Kiwanis and Lions would not let Blacks into their clubs.

8. The Rotary Club was able to spread beyond the west coast of Africa and literally impacted the continent of Africa.

9. Africans who became members of the Rotary benefitted from their training in the Club in America. They took up positions in Africa and negotiated with club members in America on economic matters.[19]

The Frontiers International still has an opportunity, in spite of the setback of a Rotary Club's stronghold on the African continent, to make a forceful impact and possible attraction of new membership on the African scene. This would legitimize the "International" title given to the organization. Even though the Frontiers falls under the auspices of "social organization," nothing, when considering relationships of countries, is a-political according to Dr. Dennis. A campaign for membership could focus on concerns like "dumping of nuclear waste, or social concerns of Black people in Africa and America" or other questions (e.g., tropical diseases) that are primary in the minds of the average African. These questions have not been touched on by groups like the Rotary.[20] "There must be," suggested Dennis, "a different need which will draw attention to the organization."[21]

In exploring an answer to the question, in which African countries where the Frontiers would have the greatest impact if the organization attempted to establish contact, Dr. Dennis agreed that some of the West African countries, e.g. Ghana and Nigeria, due to their history of western association, would be among the likely places to contact. However, he did suggest that Zimbabwe, "because of its western-American basis in terms of its outlook," and newly established independence, has helped it to become receptive to anything American.[22]

The final point, which highlights the question of a possible future for the Frontiers International in the African complex, focuses on one point -- "internationalizing the national scene." In order for the Frontiers to have an impact on Africa as an effective group on the American scene, which has met the needs of the Black population, the many young Africans now studying at American colleges and universities, in great numbers, must be invited, in an overt fashion, to become members of the of the Frontiers. Special programs for membership inclusion must be devised so that questions directly affecting the African population can be dealt with (e.g., AIDS, health care, sanitation, travel, population control, and government stabilization). Membership in America might assure the establishment of clubs in Africa when African students return to their homelands. It will also assure the building of new bridges between Black Americans and Africans. The future for the Frontiers International in this vital area of concern looks bright.[23]

NOTES

[1]<u>Frontiersman</u>, Summer 1965, vol.4 no.2, p.1.

[2]Ibid.

[3]Letter from International Office Secretary Thelma Robinson, dated 2/28/89.

[4]<u>Frontiersman</u>, Jan., Feb., Mar. 1976, vol.15, no.1, p.1.

[5]John S. Mbiti, <u>African Religions and Philosophy</u>, (N.Y.: Doubleday Anchor Books, 1969), p.282.

[6]Ibid., p.285.

[7]Ibid., p.291.

[8]Ibid., p.293.

[9]Ibid.

[10]Ibid., p.294.

[11]Ibid., p.295.

[12]Phyllis M. Martin and Patrick O'Meara, ed., <u>Africa</u>, (Ind.: Indiana Univ. Press, 1977), pp.176-177.

[13]Vera Micheles Dean, <u>The Non-Western World</u>, (N.Y.: Mentor Book, 1957), p.209.

[14]Nnamdi Azikiwe, <u>My Odyssey: An Autobiography</u>, (London: C. Hurst & Co., 1970), p.187.

[15]Kwame Nkrumah, <u>Ghana: The Autobiography of Kwame</u>

Nkrumah, (N.Y.: International Publishers, 1957), p.31.

[16]Ibid., pp.44, 45.

[17]Interview with Fred Johnson and Leonard L. Bethel, researchers, Plainfield, N.J., Thursday, March 23, 1989.

[18]Ibid.

[19]Ibid.

[20]Ibid.

[21]Ibid.

[22]Ibid.

[23]Ibid.

CHAPTER IX

SERVICE: A COMMUNITY CHALLENGE

There was no doubt that a volunteer spirit permeated the thinking and activity of Nimrod B. Allen, founder ofthe Frontiers International, Inc. His effort destroyed the myth that the Black American was always looking for a handout and that there was a tendency towards the destruction of community life rather than building it up. The first group of men who joined him in this venture were able to prove, over the years of dedication and hard work, that Black men could work together effectively toward instituting social change. Allen represented the magnetic force which drew these dedicated men together and created, as a result, a lasting spirit of community involvement through service.

In the mid-1930's life in America was difficult enough for the average American. For the Black family it meant extraordinary sacrifices, sometimes beyond human endurance. In the midst of these Depression years, however, there were sparks of hope emerging through the deprivation. The Frontiers organization was one of those sparks of hope for the Black community. However, not all went well around the country. Segregation in the South and racial discrimination in the North persisted. Some chapters of the Frontiers formed in the midst of that hysteria and survived the conflict. With the support of women organized into Frontiers Auxiliaries, the push for equality and justice had more meaning. Involvement in voter registration, volunteer efforts in feeding the hungry and poor gave a greater meaning to the volunteer, pioneering activity that took place among the men and women in the membership. There was a concerted effort to work against the odds in the performance of community service.

According to one authoritative source, Black organizations were created by "the political, social, economic and educational horizons" opened to Black people in the United States during the 20th Century.[1] Segregation, especially close social cleavages (fraternities, sororities, business clubs, secret societies, and professional clubs) helped Black Americans to find their social, political and psychological solace in the infra-structure of Black organizations.

The very first organizations for Blacks started to emerge immediately following the Civil War. In 1864 the Ancient and Accepted Scottish Rite Masons came on the scene and registered as late as 1967 some 25,000 members. In 1895, a year before the Supreme Court's ruling that justified a segregated society--The Plessy vs. Ferguson Act--and also the year in which Booker T.Washington (the most respected Negro leader of that day) delivered his famous "Atlanta Compromise" address at the cotton exposition in Atlanta, Georgia, the National Medical Association was founded. In 1898 the Improved Benevolent Protective Order of Elks of the World were established and by 1967 claimed a 500,000 membership. When the Frontiers International was founded in 1936, there were 27 such Black organizations already in place serving communities throughout the country. From 1936-1959 13 more came into existence. Their very presence on the American scene symbolized the determined effort of Black citizens that segregation would not prevent organizing and functioning on the local and national levels. Each had its own purpose and goal, but they all sent a clear message to the broader White community which said that Black Americans would not be denied the freedom to organize and serve the interests of its own people. Just a year prior to (1935) the founding of the Frontiers International, the National Council of Negro Women, founded by the distinguished educator, Mary McLeod Bethune, catapulted the idea that Black women could develop programs which would enhance the economic, social, cultural and educational welfare of Black women in society.[2] It was not difficult for the Frontiers to crystallize the notion, in 1936, of service to community by Black men and their women's auxiliaries.

Black Americans, who were intellectually stimulated and socially conscious in the early 1900's, struggled to become socially self-sufficient as members of fraternal orders and benefit associations. "Masons and Odd Fellows maintained large Negro memberships; in addition, organizations like the Knights of Pythias and the Knights of Tabor competed for membership among Negro men."[3] Furthermore, there were organizations like "the International Order of Good Samaritans, the Ancient Sons of Israel, the Grand United Order of True Reformers, and the Independent Order of St. Luke," all secret in nature (i.e., they performed their duties without publicity and exposure), who, for example, "offered insurance against sickness and death, aided widows and orphans of deceased members, and gave opportunities for social intercourse."[4] Their activities tended to be internal and acts of good will were primarily relegated to membership. A few of these secret organizations could only be found in certain localities, but some "had memberships that extended over several states and owned the buildings which housed their main offices as well as other property which they rented to Negro businesses."[5]

118

The 20th Century was a period of growth for Black organizations. The Masons and Odd Fellows, for example, "established club-houses and centers where members and friends could enjoy the fellowship that comes from association."[6]

One cannot ignore, however, some of the groundwork laid in the mid-1800's. Slavery had not ended, but Free Negroes were active in organizational structures in the Northeastern cities, as a means of social survival. They "held in high esteem their fraternal organizations and benevolent societies."[7] The Masons, for example, "continued to flourish during the generation immediately preceding the Civil War."[8] The Masons in Maryland, around 1845, formed the First Colored Grand Lodge. "In 1843, under the leadership of Peter Ogden, a group of free Negroes organized the Grand United Order of Odd Fellows, which became one of the major Negro fraternal organizations."[9] The need to bind themselves together for "social and cultural uplift, economic advancement, and mutualized relief" became social and psychological incentives for the Free Negro population. Large numbers of benevolent societies came into existence to fulfill these purposes. Between 1821 and 1840 organizations like The Friendship Benevolent Society for Social Relief; the Star in the East Association; and the Daughters of Jerusalem "were some of the more prominent organizations with substantial savings accounts in Baltimore banks."[10] Moreover, it was historically significant that in those cities where Free Negroes existed in any number, "there were benevolent associations of mechanics, coachmen, chaulkers, and other workers" which suggested that Blacks were "organizing themselves into unions at about the same time as the Whites."[11]

The social behavior of the early Black fraternal organizations which came out of the slavery and Reconstrucion periods laid solid ground for an organization like the Frontiers International. Emerging in the midst of the Depression years in 1936 brought new challenges and goals. It, therefore, tended to take on a different posture as it related to the Black community. Its activity was not so much internally focused as early fraternal groups. Even though the newly established Black Greek organizations (e.g. Alpha Kappa Alpha, Delta Sigma Theta, Zeta Phi Beta, Alpha Phi Alpha, Kappa Alpha Psi, and Phi Beta Sigma) had social agendas to meet the needs of the Black community (e.g., raising scholarship money for needy Black students to attend college and helping the elderly and disabled), the social infra-structure and initiation practices made their general focus somewhat different than the focus of the Frontiers International. The latter's total commitment, both internally and externally, was based on service to the local community. There were no initiation rites that were secret in nature, no hidden handshakes and signs or symbols. Their intent was community service only. However, their social gatherings and fellowship solidified a strong sense of comradery and togetherness. Membership meant a word of dedication to service and formal induction. The paying of dues and fund raising were instruments to carry out its program to help those needy in community life. The key to the Frontiers' function as an organization was embodied in its motto, "Advancement Through Service." The giving of time, resources and talents embodied its program of activity and many people, in every city where the Frontiers were located, benefitted from the efforts of dedicated Black men and women (auxiliary members).

Another unique aspect of the Frontiers' activity was that its program of service was different from community to community, pending the social needs. Even though there were a few nationally focused programs, such as the Vitiligo Foundation, individual needs, especially in the minority community, were given special attention from city to city.

In an age when Black men have been suspect, in every community in America, as not being productive or concerned about progress, Black men in the Frontiers clubs across the country have proven, since 1936, that serving the community was commonplace, usually unrecognized by local news media. They tended to be men and women from the professional world (teachers, businessmen, politicians, clergy and philanthropists) and the work-a-day world (truck drivers, laborers and housewives). They also tended not to be people who were not in the habit of getting local, state or federal and private organizational support. They tended to raise their own resources through dues and projects. The image of self-help was commonplace and a sense of gratification permeated each club after scholarships were awarded to needy college students, donations were made to service organizations like the YMCA, YWCA, Boy Scouts, Girl Scouts, and hospital and medical institutions.

In his book, Black Bourgeoisie, E. Franklin Frazier, noted Black scholar, was highly critical of Black business organizations that proclaimed self-sufficiency without making connection with larger White institutions. He probably frowned on Black organizations like the Frontiers, which, over the years, tested the abilities and desires of its own membership to be self-sufficient. He quoted, for example, a Professor Harris in the latter's work, The Negro as Capitalist: ". . . the Negro masses, urged by theirleaders, were led to place increasing faith in business and property as a means of escaping poverty and achieving economic independence. Although ostensibly sponsored as the means of self-help or racial cooperation. . . ."[12] Frazier saw this behavior as a form of myth that prevented real progress. He said, for example, "The myth of Negro business is fed by the false notions and values that are current in the isolated social world of the Negro, a world dominated by the views and mental outlook of the black bourgeoisie."[13]

Even though some of Dr. Frazier's ideas were a serious contribution to scholarship and a challenge to the Black community in general, he and those who frown on Black self-help organizations, failed to capture the great success of an organization like the Frontiers International who were able to capture the best Black talent at the local community levels and at the same time expound the highest form of communication and diplomacy with the community-at-large. Even though, at the social and psychological levels, the Frontiers were Black in structure, at the broader political, economic, medical, and educational levels, Yokefellows (name for Frontiersmen) and Yokettes (name for women's auxiliary) have always been diplomats and couriers of goodwill and humanitarian advocacy, it was at this level that the reputation of social excellence was won for the Frontiers International an enduring future of strength and solidarity as an organization. It also serves as a beacon of hope for a Black community in need of strong, positive images for Black youth and adults who need social, psychological and spiritual uplift. The Frontiers motto lives on -- "Advancement Through Service."

NOTES

[1]Harry A. Ploski, and Roscoe C. Brown, Jr., ed. , The Negro Almanac, (N.Y.: Bellwether Publishing Co., Inc., 1967), p. 817.

[2]Ibid. p. 821.

[3]John Hope Franklin, From Slavery to Freedom, (N.Y.: Alfred A. Knopf, 1956), p. 399.

[4]Ibid.

[5]Ibid.

[6]Ibid, P. 552.

[7]Ibid, p. 223.

[8]Ibid.

[9]Ibid. pp. 223-224.

[10]Ibid, p. 224.

[11]Ibid.

[12]Ibid

[13]Ibid.

123A
Founder & President Emeritus.
Nimrod B. Allen
Oct. 12 1886, to Dec. 15, 1977

123B
Frontiers Executive Secretary, Harold L. Pilgrim and Patricia Harris, HUD Secretary at the 4th Annual HUD-Service Clubs Conference, held Jan. 27 & 28, 1977 in Washington, D.C. in Washington, D.C.

123C
Frontiers Eastern Regional Conference at Philadelphia, PA., 1954. Standing (left), Dr. Bernard Harris of Baltimore, Md., International President 1952-54 and 1956-58. Standing Standing right, Nimrod B. Allen, Founder of Frontiers Int.

124A
International Convention, Akron, Ohio
7-29-61. (left to right) Harold L.
Pilgrim, Exec. Sec., Randall C. Morgan,
Int'l Pres., 1960-62, and Marcus
Neustadter, Jr., Int'l Pres., 1964-66.

124B
Seated (left to right) Nimrod B. Allen,
Founder of Frontiers Int'l and James F.
King, Int'l Pres., 1962-64.
Standing (left) Marcus Neustadter, Jr.,
Int'l Pres. 1964-66, and (right Dr.
Hubert B. Crouche, Int'l Pres. 1966-67.

124C
President Clarence A. Dockens (right), Int'l Pres., 1967-69, presenting Hamilton Watch to
Nimrod B. Allen, Founder, at executive committee meeting in Columbus, Ohio, Oct. 21,
1967.

Southwest District Conference, Holiday Inn, Houston, Texas, 1975.
Bottom Row (L to R) Rev. Arthur Livingston; Jerome McNeil; Collie Chambers of the
Houston Club, Dr. Malcolm D. Williams, Int'l Pres., 1975-77; Rev. Dr. Phale Hale,
Congressman, Columbus, Ohio, and Frontiers Int'l Pres., 1969-70; A. J. Dickerson,
Southwest District Director and member of the Houston Club. Leroy Murray and Mack H.
Hannah, Jr., also of the Houston Club.
Top Row (L to R) Willie Clemmons, Louisiana State Director of Frontiers; M. C. Henry,
President of the Houston Club; Willie Iles and E. Williams of the Houston Club; Jesse
Prudhomme; Andrew Dartez of Opelousas, La., William Merritt, Houston Club; Leon
Guillory, Opelousas; Rev. C. Anderson Davis and Willie Jefferson, Houston Club.

125B

(5th From left) Andrew "Boots" Johnson was Int'l. Pres., 1970 to Feb 1972.

126A

State Dept. Conference in Washington, D.C., Sept. 18, 1973. (left to right) Clyde D. Mitchell, Int'l Pres., Feb.1972-July 1973; William S. Blair Jr., Dep. Secretary of the Army for Public Affairs; and Harold L. Pilgrim, Frontiers Exec. Secretary.

126B

Dr. & Mrs. Charles A. Moore, Jr. Moore was Int'l Pres., 1973-75.

126C

1978

(left to right) Elmer C. Jackson, Jr., Esq. (Frontiers Legal Counsel) receives Frontiers Int'l Service Award from International President Rudolph Hampton, 1977-1979.

126D

Wilbert F. Singleton (left), Int'l Pres., 1979-81, presents Frontier's annual Vitiligo Center contribution to Yokefellow Dr. John A. Kenney, Jr., Chairman, Dept. of Dermatology, Howard Univ., Wash, D.C., while 1st Vice-Pres. Robert K. Hill looks on.

127A

(left) Int'l Pres. Robert K. Hill (1981-83) and Int'l Pres. Dale G. Lee (1985-87) with their wives at the Williamsburg, Va. convention, 1986.

127B

(left) Int'l Pres. Guy A. Jones (1983-85) congratulates Robert L. Johnson, Director of Vitilgo Foundation, succeeding Emmer M. Lancaster, July, 1984.

127C

1987

(left) Bill Joiner, Int'l Pres., 1987-89 confers with Leonard Coleman, New Jersey Commissioner of Community Affairs.

127D

Floyd W. Alston, Int'l Pres., 1989-

The Philadelphia Club, December, 1946. In the front row, fifth from the left, is the celebrated black poet, Langston Hughes.

128B
Frontiers Club of Philadelphia - 1964

128C
The Rev. Thomas W. S. Logan, Sr., Int'l Chaplain. (A 1946 photo.)

Convention Delegates, 1973- Harrisburg, PA

129B
Yokefellow A. J. Dickerson, 5th District
Director (Texas) presents Frontiers
Distinguished Service Award to the
Honorable Barbara C. Jordan,
Congresswoman from Texas, at the
Frontiers International Convention in
Atlantic City, N.J., July, 1975.

129C
Guest Speaker Roy Wilkens (left)
Executive Director of the NAACP and
Malcolm D. Williams, Int'l Pres. of
Frontiers at Wash., D.C., Frontiers
Convention, July 1976.

130A
At Executive Committee Meeting, 1977
(left to right) Seated: Herbert Wise,
Int'l Treasurer; Sara W. Dickerson,
Pres., Womens Auxiliary; Dr. Malcolm
Williams, Int'l Pres.; Felton Alexander,
Int'l Treasurer.
Standing: (left to right) Rudolph
Hampton, International 1st Vice
President, Dr. Charles A. Moore,
International Immediate Past President,
George Wilkes, Gary and Bill Joiner,
Seventh District Director.

130B
Frontiers International Convention,
Nashville, Tenn., 1977
(left) Guest Speaker, Former
Yokefellow Benjamin L. Hooks,
Federal Communications Commissioner
and NAACP Exec. Dir. & Nimrod B.
Allen, Founder of Frontiers.

130C
Mrs. Francine B. Freeman, Int'l
President of Coordinating Council of
Women's Auxiliaries, 1978.

130D
Rev. H. Albion Ferrell, 1978 Former
International
Chaplain

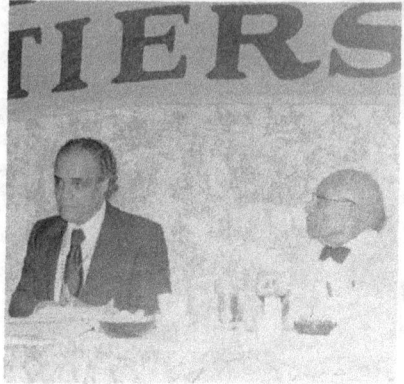

131A

Yokefellow A. Leon Higgenbotham, Jr., Appellate Court Judge and author of "In the Matter of Color" poses with Yokette Claudine Snowden of Baltimore at a Frontiers "Get-To-Gether"

131B

Convention: Omaha, Nebr., 1983 (Seated left to right) George Alford, Int'l Sgt.-at-Arms, Mrs. Roberta Alford, Pres., Coordinating Council Aux., 1980-81, Mrs. Lena Snead, former Int'l Treas., Coordinating Council, and James Snead, Chairman Int'l Budget Proposal Committee.

131C

(left to right) Yokette Cleo Turner, President of the Frontiers Coordinating Council, 1983-84; Yokefellow Dr. Harold R. Minus, Chairman, Dept. of Dermatology, Howard Univ., Wash., D.C., succeeding Dr. John Kenney, Jr.; and Yokefellow Robert L. Johnson, Vitilgo Foundation Director, 1984

131D

1986

Wilbur E. Hobbs (left), Pres. of the Philadelphia Frontiers accepts Club Award from Robert L. Johnson, Admin. Dir., Vitilgo Foundation, Inc.

132A

Yokefellow Clinton Rose has just unveiled the bust of Duke Ellington on the stage of the Performing Arts Center in Milwaukee. He is flanked by the sculptress Dr. Selma Burke and Mercer Ellington, the Duke's oldest son. July, 1987, Frontiers Convention.

132B

Oct. 28, 1988
(left to right) Frontiers Newark Club Pres., Rev. Willie Simmons; Mrs. Pearlena Jackson, Vitilgo disease patient; the Honorable Sharp James, Mayor of Newark, N.J.; Yokefellow Frederick Stalks, First District Medical Research Chairman; and Frontiers Int'l Sgt.-at-Arms, George Alford.

132C

(left to right) Dr. John A. Kenney, Jr.; Congressman Parren J. Mitchell of Maryland; Int'l Pres., Malcolm D. Williams; and Emmer M. Lancaster discuss the "Mitchell Bill" concerning Vitilgo and N.I.H.

132D

Mrs. Thelma E. Robinson, Former Office Mgr., Frontiers Int'l.

BIBLIOGRAPHY

Alexander, Mack. The Kansas City Star. 1974.

Allen, Nimrod B. Crisis: A Record of The Darker Races. vol. 24. 1922.

Annual Reports. Frontiers: Phila., 1978-79.

Azikiwe, Nnamdi. My Odyssey: An Autobiography. London: C. Hurst
& Co., 1970.

Boone, William A. Ebony. Chicago: Johnson Publishing Co. 1962.

Brown, Mary C. letter dated October 22, 1986.

Brown, Roscoe C. and Harry A. Ploski. ed. The Negro Almanac.
N.Y. Bellwether Publishing Co., Inc. 1967.

Cade, Toni. ed. The Black Woman. N.Y.: Signet Books, 1970.

Certificate of Incorporation District of Columbia. March, 1954.

Club reports: Gary, Ind.; Harrisburg, Pa.; Newark, NJ; Decatur,
Ga. ; Nashville, Tenn.; Milwaukee, Wisc.; Tallahassee, Fla.

Conventions: July 20-24, 1975, Holiday Inn; 35th, July 25-30,
Hyatt Regency Hotel, Washington, D.C.; 37th, July 1978, Forum
Thirty Hotel, Springfield, Ill.; August 1963, Sheraton-
Blackstone Hotel, Chicago, Ill.; 31st Annual, Springfield,
Ohio.

Coordinating Council. Women's Auxiliaries of the Frontiers
International. Constitution (revised 1976).

Dean, Vera Micheles. The Non-Western World. N.Y.: Mentor Book
1957.

Dees Jr., Jesse Walter The College Built on Prayer: Mary McLeod
Bethune. N.Y.: Ganis and Harris. 1953.

Dickerson, Sara. historical statement, Houston, Texas. 1986.

Fletcher, Alma J. President of Philadelphia Auxiliary, a letter dated October 8, 1986.

Foster, A.L. The Competitor. vol. II. Issue 1 , pp. 9-12.

Fountain, Odessa. President, Newark, N.J. Auxiliary. A letter statement dated February 29, 1987.

Franklin, John Hope. From Slavery to Freedom. N.Y.: Alfred A. Knopf. 1956.

Frontiers pamphlet reports: 31st Annual Convention, Springfield, Ohio, 1971 ; Eta Omicron Zeta Chapter, Zeta Phi Beta Sorority, Inc., report (undated); Manual for Local Clubs, Part X, Sect. 4, 1977.

Frontiersman. newsletter, vol. 15, Number 2, April, May, June 1978, p.4. col. l.

. Summer 1965. vol. 4. no.2. p.1.

. Jan., Feb., Mar. 1976. vol. 15. no.1.

Giddings, Paula. In Search of Sisterhood: Delta Sigma Theta and the Challenge of the Black Sorority Movement. N.Y.: William Morrow and Co., Inc. 1988.

Hall, Richard H. Organizations: Structures and Process. N.J.: Prentice-Hall, Inc. 1982.

Henderson, Stephen. Understanding the New Black Poetry. N.Y.: William Morrow & Co., Inc. 1973.

Henning, Margaret and Anne Jardin. N.Y.: Pocket Books, 1978.

Interviews: Frederick Johnson and Leonard Bethel. Thursday, March 23,1989; Pearlena E. Jackson, Newark, N.J., Jan. 1987.

Jeffries, Bettye W. President, Auxiliary, Tallahassee, Fla., Little Rock, Ark., October, 1986.

Lancaster, Emmer Martin. pamphlet statement. Washington, D.C. June 9, 1950.

Letters: International Office, secretary - Thelma Robinson,
Feb. 28, 1989; Josephine Hargis, Treasurer, Auxiliary,
Williamsburg, Va. 1987; Annie B. Nelson, President,
Auxiliary, Tallahassee, Fla., Oct. 11, 1986; Claudine
Snowden, Baltimore, Md. Auxiliary, Oct. 14, 1986.

Martin, Phyllis M. and Patrick O'Meara, ed. Africa. Ind.:
Indiana Univ. Press. 1977.

Mbiti, John S. African Religions and Philosophy. N.Y.:
Doubleday Anchor Books, 1969.

Motley, JoAnne. statement, Canton, Ohio. July 9, 1986.

National Frontiers Vitiligo Foundation, Inc. "Annual Report",
June 30, 1986.

National Institute of Health, March 1977.

Nkrumah, Kwame. Ghana: The Autobiography. London: C. Hurst and
Co., 1970.

Pamphlets: NAUW (undated); Zeta Phi Beta Sorority, Inc.   (undated).

Report on elected officials, 1986.

Smith, Dorothy E. statement, Springfield, Ill., Oct. 15, 1986.

The Tennessean. May 20, 1968; August 7, 1968; July 25,1977;
February 10, 1971; March 1968; July 30, 1962.

U.S. Department of Health and Human Services, NIH Publ. no.80-
2088, July 1980.

Warriner, Charles K. Organizations and Their Environments. Conn.:
Jai Press Inc., 1984.

Weare, Walter B. Black Business in the New South. Chicago:
Univ. of Ill. Press. 1973.

Whitaker, Marjorie. Bricks Tri-county Auxiliary, Feb. 3, 1987.

Woods, Armell G. Saginaw, Mich., July, 1986.

INDEX

A

"Advance Through Service", 15

African scene, 109-118
letter from Kenya, 110-11
impact of Rotary on Africa, 116-117

Allen, Alexander J., 5

Allen, Nimrod B., 1-7

Alpha Kappa Alpha, 10

Ancient Sons of Israel, 1

Annapolis, Maryland Club, 30

Annual Conventions, 7, 8, 3, 33, 34

Ashby, William, 35

Auxiliary clubs, 0

Azikiwe, Nnamdi, 114

B

Baton Rouge Frontiers Club, Louisiana, 31

Berry, John L., 5

Bethune, Mary McLeod, 1

Big Brother, 19

Big Sister, 19

Black Bourgeoisie
(E.Franklin Frazier), 14

Black Greek organizations AKA,Delta, Zeta, Alpha,Kappa,Sigma, 13

Black organizations
(a listing) , 98-101

Black Woman (Toni Cade Bambara), 7

Bratcher, M.F., 3

C

Cain, C.M., 5

Campbell, Earl E., 4

Campbell, Edna O.G., 77

Canton, Ohio Club, 38

Caribbean scene, 109

Carter, Dr.J.J., 3

Chartered members, 1

Chartered women's auxiliaries, 74

Cheek, Thomas, 9

Chicago Club, 31

"Colored Masons" movement, 105

Columbus Club, 1

136

Index

Frederick, Maryland Club, 31

Index

Index

Index

V

Vitiligo, 19, 61-68
  Pearlena E. Jackson of
    Newark, N.J., 61-6
  dermatologists (Dr.'s
    William Anderson, John
    Kenney, Harold Minus,
    and Pearl Grimes), 6
  autoimmune reaction, 63
  Vitiligo Foundation, 65, 67
  Howard University College of
    Medicine, 66
      University support: Yale,
      Howard, Bryn Mawr, U. of
      Penn., U. of Mass., and
      Mass. Eye and Ear Infirmary
      of Boston, Mass., 66
  FIFI, 68

W

Whittaker, Forest F.,

Williams, J.W., 3

Wiseman, Rose S., 80

Women's auxiliaries, 75-90
  Philadelphia, Pa., 75-77;
  Baltimore, Md., 77-80;
  Annapolis, Md., 80-81; Houston,
  Texas, 81-82; Newark, N.J., 82-
  83; Bricks Tri-county, 83-84;
  Decatur, Ill., 84-85; Springfield,
  Ill., 85; Williamsburg, Va.,
  86; Tallahassee, Fla., 86-87; Little
  Rock, Ark., 87-88; Canton, Ohio,
  88-89; Akron, Ohio, 89;
  Milwaukee, Wis., 90; Saginaw,
  Mich., 90

Y

YMCA, 19, 14

YWCA, 19, 14

Yokettes, 76

Z

Zeta Phi Beta, 103

9 780761 859734